Awakening Your Inner Radiance with LifeForce Yoga

Strategies for Coping with Depression, Anxiety, & Trauma

ROSE KRESS, ERYT-500, C-IAYT

DEDICATION

For my husband Tom.
Thank you for your unending love and support.
I could not have done this without you.

CONTENTS

ACKNOWLEDGMENTS

Thank you and all the love to my husband Tom. You are always there, you catch me when I fall, and you hold me when I need it. I am so blessed to be on this journey through life with you.

Thanks and love to my family – Andrea, Jonathan, Rush, Anton Virginia, Erin, Aiden, and Catalina. I would not be here without you.

Thanks to Amy Weintraub for introducing me, and the world, to LifeForce Yoga. You spent many years teaching me and laying the foundation for the teacher that I have become.

Thank you to my cheerleading squad – Jeremiah Webb, Jamie Cieplinski, Ginny Beal, Merrill Black, Kathleen Williams, Alyce Wellons, Liz Payne, Dawn Browning, Wendy Humphreys, Brittany Weber and John Goforth. Your notes, videos, texts, and messages kept me going.

Special thanks to Jeremiah Webb for 23 years of friendship, countless experiences, laughing until there are no words, and ALL the gummies! You ARE family.

To my P.I.C. (partner in crime) Ginny Beal, for a long and fruitful friendship full of laughter, yoga, spiritual growth, and sticking together.

Thanks to Tori Amos. Years ago, you told me to "outcreate the darkness." I took that message to heart and it has been guiding me through personal moments of darkness and the global darkness. Your music provided the soundtrack to my writing.

Thank you to Brandon Asraf and John Tacon of Brick + Mortar for the tunes! Your music lifts me up like and is the soundtrack to my mental health. I have dreams of a mental health collaboration.

Thank you to Wendy and James Humphreys of Pacific Yew Yoga (www.pacificyewyoga.com) for providing me with a yoga home in the Pacific North West and the use of the studio for the photographs. I knew there was something special about the studio from the moment I saw the name. I have such deep gratitude to you both for the community you have created and welcomed me into.

Thank you to Spencer Smith for your skilled photography, putting up with my forgetful texts, and making me look good!

Thank you to my teachers. Rama Jyoti Vernon, your wisdom is unmatched. Maria Mendola, your sweetness is unparalleled.

Thank you to Elena Brower for your guidance and inspiration. I have only been on this dōTERRA journey with you for a year and yet it seems like forever.

A very special thank you to the all the LifeForce Yoga Practitioners and ALL my students! You are an inspiration. <3

INTRODUCTION

Inner Radiance is the experience of being connected with the part of you that is unsullied by the constrictions of life. It is your expanded and limitless consciousness that is your true nature. Inner Radiance is another expression for the Transcendental Self, Divine essence, God Consciousness, the eternal cosmic vibration, or the Universe. The light of your Inner Radiance is always shining, even when it is occluded by the clouds of depression, anxiety, and trauma. This manual is a guide to help you uncover the pathways to your Inner Radiance and allow it to shine in all areas of your life.

What you hold in your hands is the culmination of decades of work and thousands of years of wisdom. LifeForce Yoga began informally in 1989 when Amy Weintraub sought to support her mental health with a yoga practice. Through study, personal practice, trainings, and working with others Amy discovered techniques that helped to lift the fog of depression. If you have not read her first book, <u>Yoga for Depression</u>, I highly recommend it.

In 2002, I discovered Amy's class at the Tucson Racquet and Fitness Club. By 2004, Amy had a CD and a book, and a training program. I came on board after my yoga teacher training in 2005 as an assistant and eventually became the Education Director for LifeForce Yoga and managed the trainings. In 2016, I purchased LifeForce Yoga. All these years later, we still work together, albeit in a very diminished capacity as Amy is shifting to writing fiction. At this writing, her book <u>Temple Dancer</u>, is slated for publication.

In some ways I feel that I have always been practicing yoga. I remember doing things like legs up the wall in my bed when I was feeling funky. I liked to be upside down and I still do although it is not possible in the same way. When I was young and suffering from insomnia, I began a practice of relaxing my body from the toes up; I always fell asleep before I got to my shoulders. I also remember having an epiphany around my own reverse breathing pattern when I was 12 or 13. It seems that I was always on this path.

Our stories are always changing…evolving. They are the foundation of who we are. But we are not our stories; we are so much more.

My story begins in the late 70s. I was born on January 5th, the same day as the great yogi Paramahansa Yoganananda. Upon finding this out, I have taken this to be auspicious. I come from a blended family, I have an older half-brother and two younger siblings. On my maternal side, both of my grandparents were immigrants that assimilated well. On my paternal side, we have been here since the Revolutionary War. We are a family generic white people who bury their emotions, what I like to call "fineaholics." But for me, those emotions were explosive, they would not stay buried. For this I suffered…greatly.

My first feeling memory is being with my nanny in the dining room during a thunderstorm. I was frightened and my parents were not there. A thunderstorm in Southern Arizona is something to behold. The lightning shows are spectacular and the thunder booms across the desert. I can say this as an adult that is in the process of healing. But as a child, thunderstorms terrified me. At the first sound of thunder, my bowels would loosen, and I had to race to the bathroom. I was so embarrassed about this and did everything I could to hide it and it lasted into my 20s. I felt shame at being so anxious over a natural phenomenon, when no one else had this reaction. I guess that you could say this was my first trauma.

Like everyone, my childhood had traumas. Unlike everyone, I developed post-traumatic stress disorder (PTSD) from it. My childhood is filled with feelings of anger, resentment, blame, anxiety, panic, and shame. I cried every day until I was 12. I felt trapped and alone with no real way to express those feelings. All I wanted was to not be a child. I thought that being an adult with freedom would change everything.

It didn't. I was always anxious, I didn't sleep well, I suffered from nightmares, and I had obsessive compulsive disorder. At 17, I began having severe panic attacks and was diagnosed with a clinical depression. I went on medication and felt normal again, a normal anxious, angry, and resentful teenager.

In relationship, I began to heal. It was very slow. I learned to trust and to be happy. I felt attached to Tom and that was so healing for me (we are together all these years later). I even started to enjoy the lightning and thunder shows. But I was still so anxious. I washed my hands a bazillion times a day. I could not touch things in public without feeling dirty. I had to check the locks on the door all the time. I still had a hard time sleeping. Even though I had my freedom and was with someone that loved me and that I loved, I was still deeply unhappy.

And then I found LifeForce Yoga and Amy Weintraub. My first yoga class was in 1994 and I had practiced it in some form for the eight years before going to the first class with Amy. I went because I had felt better when I did it in the past. My body felt uncomfortable, my hips were tight and my middle back hurt where the scoliosis was. I had never talked about them because that is not what you do when "everything is fine." I thought that making a change would make me feel better. I was in college and I got up at 5:30am to go to yoga class three times a week. I could barely make it to an 8am class, but I was on my mat by 6:40am for years.

After that first class, I remember walking onto campus for my first class. I passed under the Eucalyptus tree and I was overwhelmed with the smell of it. I had never smelled those trees that way. It was such an awe-inspiring feeling. At that moment, I knew there was something special about this weird yoga class that was filled with breathing practices, sounds, and a strange lady that talked about the practices in terms of alleviating depression.

To be honest, when I started the class, I went because there was a man on the schedule. I had never done yoga with a male teacher and I thought I might try it. When I walked into the room, this small woman walked up to me and said, "Hi! I'm Amy, what's your name?" I responded and thought, "well geez, I can't leave now." So, I stayed, figuring that I would go to the man's class the next time. Within the first 5 minutes of class, I knew that I had found what I was looking for. Even though I did not make it to his class, Tom Beall became one of my teacher trainers in my Yoga Training.

Over the years, the practice worked on me. I became calmer, the compulsions lessened, and I started to sleep better. It was so gradual that I did not really notice it. I started working for Amy and eventually became a yoga teacher. I began to understand my suffering better. Things rose to the surface and then passed through me. I wasn't so reactive or angry anymore.

2010 was a watershed year for me. I hosted a training with my friend Ginny Beal. During the training we were sensing into physical sensations. I had been ignoring that pain behind my heart, because it was just always there. Finally, I let my partner in the experience guide me into that feeling. As I sensed into it, a deep grief came up over a loss at age 5. I saw how I had put every grief or feeling that I could not handle into my body. For over 20 years, I had been stuffing my emotions into my back because I just did not know what to do with them. That evening I had a massive unburdening and letting go. I sobbed and cried like I was having a tantrum. I felt better after that.

The next day, I felt different. Everything seemed new. It was like I had been given a new outlook. I felt that way for months, I guess until I became used to it and I forgot how I viewed the world before. The anxiety was gone. The compulsions were gone. The anger was gone. I slept with ease. All the yoga I had done had set me up for this deep clearing of old traumas in one moment. All the yoga that I continued to do was keeping me clear.

After that, I thought my story with anxiety was done. Sure, there were moments where I would get anxious in a situation, but that happens to everyone. In those moments, I used my LifeForce Yoga tools and then I was calm again. I had tools for keeping me balanced and even. I grew. Emotionally I was stable. I was in my 30s and I was on an even keel. No big deal.

On November 15th, 2017, I was rear-ended at a stop light. The injuries from this accident are still ongoing. The aftermath left me with anxiety and an emotional roller coaster. Some days the emotions were barely manageable. They rose like a swollen river and overflow their banks. I was anxious beyond reckoning and even had panic attacks for the first time in decades. Hopelessness moved in and it was soul crushing. Some days I could not see a way out and thought that I would just give everything up and disappear.

In my 40s, I am relearning who I am, because we never really stay the same. We all grow, and we all change. While life may change in a moment, for many these changes are without a brain injury. The fallout from the head trauma and injuries led to navigating a different body and mind. It takes time to figure things out. It is a scary roller coaster. The practices that once worked needed to be replaced because this damaged nervous system cannot handle them anymore. Yoga classes are more challenging than ever – it is hard to go to a class when you cannot lie down on your back anymore, or when the teacher is frightened of your injuries and limitations.

Through this hopelessness, is the seed of light and hope that is my Inner Radiance. The practice and tools helped me rediscover the connection to this radiance. This ever-changing life has so much to teach and I have so much to learn. And that is the point of this life, always relearning and rediscovering the pathways to my true nature. I am whole and deeply connected.

And, we have agreed (consciously or subconsciously) on a social construct that involves work, belongings, entertainment, etc. We get distracted by the construct. We start to put things and status above experience. We define ourselves by our sufferings, by who we once were. We suffer because we will not be that person again. We forget who we really are. Each one of us is a luminous being and we are all ultimately free.

Just like our stories, life is constantly changing. We are never the same from one moment to the next. Some moments are so dramatic and intense that they change everything about us. They end who we were and start a new existence for us. Our job is to ride these waves without clinging to the shore; to understand that we are buoyant. There will be storms with big waves that overwhelm, just as there are calm seas. The more we can find and nourish our wholeness, the easier we will ride those waves.

My hope in sharing this story and the other stories from my in this book is to help you rediscover the pathways to your Inner Radiance.

Beginnings

This book started its life as a training manual. Or perhaps, better put, the training manual was the inspiration for this book. I had been looking for a way to update the practices in the manual we use and share it with the world. In June of 2019, I received a download of sorts. The outline presented itself to me in a flurry or ink and pages. It would follow the format of our training programs, but it would not include the research, which is always changing and updating. I made a conscious choice to not cover the research and to leave this as a manual for personal exploration. If research is something you desire, head over to pubmed.gov for all peer reviewed publications on yoga.

Other Ways of Knowing

In May of 2019, I had the pleasure of meeting Pat McCabe, Woman Stands Shining, a global peace activist. We were having a conversation and she mentioned "other ways of knowing." I stopped the conversation and asked her to say more. European and white culture dictates that a child is free to play, sing, dance, imagine, and explore the world in whatever the way they want, until the age of five. Then children must put away all that play and learn the world through the scientific method. But there are other ways of knowing things, through intuition, faith, reason, emotion, the senses, imagination, memory, and experience, to name a few. We get caught up in the scientific method because that is what we are taught. I invite you to experience the practices in this book from these other ways of knowing.

I want to be very clear that I am not discounting science nor the scientific method. It is one way of knowing things. 50 years ago, a yogi might tell you that certain breathing practices help to control the stress response, yet there was no research that validated this information. We do not need science to tell us how we feel or what works.

The problem with research and yoga is that there are so many variables. How do we properly isolate a yoga practice for research when we struggle to determine where yoga starts and ends? I invite you to do your due diligence and look up some of the research, while you explore the practices within the laboratory of your own mind and body. The variables within you are immeasurable, it can be difficult to know what will work for you. There are some practices for which there is no research, like Pulling Prāna, Power Hara, or Mudrās. Other practices have a lot of research on them, like Alternate Nostril Breathing or Bee Breath.

What is Yoga?

Yoga comes from the root word *yuj*, which means "to yoke." The word yoga can be defined as union. But the union of what? The union of the mind and body, the soul and the body, the ego with the higher consciousness, physical reality with limitless reality, and/or the personality with the Inner Radiance. The potential words are endless to describe this reunification. The Yoga Sūtras of Patañjali state, *yogas chitta vrtti nirodah*, which means, "yoga is to still the waves of the mind." But what is the mind?

What is LifeForce Yoga?

It is yoga, plain and simple. The practices that follow are meant to free our prāna, defined as life force, that is constricted by depressions, anxieties, and traumas. When our life force is free, we can connect with our Inner Radiance. We call it LifeForce Yoga because we are sharing a focused methodology of balancing the mood and emotions through yogic practices. The name helps to differentiate LifeForce Yoga from other forms of yoga that may focus on body posture, exercise, stretching, or resting.

Yogic Understanding of the Mind

The mind is the realm in which most people spend their time. The Yoga Sūtras of Patanjali speak about the mind in four parts. Understanding how the mind works, according to yoga, can help us to unlock how our experiences establish our moods. Since knowledge is power, we can begin to free the mind from its endless cycles of constriction.

1. *Manas* (ma-nas) the conscious mind. This is the part of the mind that receives the sensory input from the world. It sorts all the impressions received and then sends them to the appropriate place. We can think of manas as the brain.

2. *Chitta* (chi-tah), the storehouse of the mind. This is the subconscious mind, *cit* means "to collect." It is the part of the mind that holds the patterns of behavior, known as *samsakāras*.

3. *Ahamkāra* (ah-hum-car-ra), the I-maker. This is the ego. The ahamkāra is the part of the mind that takes information from manas and calculates, compares, judges, and reacts, all while remaining in a state of separation. It sees differences and feel inferior or superior. The ahamkāra is also the preserving force of our life force and functioning in this world, for better or worse. It keeps you from stepping in front of oncoming traffic and may push you too far in a yoga pose because it may view postures as self-worth and preservation.

4. *Buddhi* (boo-dhee), the intellect or the over-mind. This is the part of the mind that reasons, creates, and holds the larger picture. The buddhi mind is a powerful state of consciousness that observes and is the witness consciousness. It is also known as the "higher mind"

Interaction of the 4 States of Mind

If the chitta is filled with negative impressions, this taints the ego, which then craves unhealthy attachments. This imbalance leads to the intellect, buddhi mind, becoming subservient to the ego and judgement becomes clouded. As the intellect becomes impaired, integration is hindered, leading to the unclear function of manas, the senses.

How This Book Works

This book serves as part memoir and part exploratory manual. Each chapter begins with a story from my own life about how yoga has supported me in relieving a constriction. There are practices and self-inquiry questions/writing prompts for you in each chapter.

We start with setting the sacred container for practice and the importance of filling your cup in a world where an empty cup can seem like a badge of honor. We will also meet the models for self-discovery on this journey. You will also be invited to set up a sacred space for your daily practice.

Chapter Two is all about welcoming intention. This goes beyond a simple intention into the sacred and spiritual intention that is *sankalpa* in yoga. Your heart's deepest desire for your growth and well-being is the jumping off point for your practice. This journey is all about you and no one else. When you listen to your heart, you will find the guidance that you seek.

Bhāvanā is the practice of cultivating an attitude that brings you closer to your Inner Radiance. This chapter introduces the LifeForce Yoga practice of bhāvanā which brings together imagination, movement, breath, and sound to actualize the emotions or states that you wish to cultivate in your life.

Chapter Four picks up the previous chapter's exploration of sound. We can calm the nervous system with the breath, but when we add sound the effect is amplified. As one

LifeForce Yoga Practitioner said, "mantra, it's like breathing, only louder." Sacred sound is a hallmark of the LifeForce Yoga practice, enhancing meditation, yoga postures, intentions, affirmations, and more.

Understanding your mood is covers some of the more complicated concepts from yoga. If we want to create long lasting change in the mood, it is important to understand our mood. This chapter presents the concepts of life force, the five bodies, constrictions, and the mood from a yogic perspective. You will learn how to identify your mood beyond the diagnostic labels of western medicine.

Chapters Six and Seven explore the constrictions of depressive and anxious energy. Techniques that meet the mood and then balance the mood are offered for practice and exploration. Practices are followed by self-inquiry questions and writing prompts to help you better understand how the techniques land within your body and mind.

Destination beingness is the discovery of balance and integration. We discuss practices that balance as well as meditation. This chapter also covers the LifeForce Yoga Chakra Clearing Meditation, a complete practice for meeting the mood, balancing, and integration. Once learned, this technique provides an opportunity to settle into a space for meditation without frustration.

Chapter Nine discusses the difficult topic of trauma from the perspective of yoga. It is not within the scope of this book to offer education around the nuances of trauma. Rather, this chapter offers techniques for health boundaries, a breathing practice, and the ultimate yogic practice.

Bringing it all together invites you to live the empowered life of which you have been dreaming. Ample self-inquiry/writing prompts support you in identifying what is needed to help you build your daily practice and commitment. This chapter includes a review, in list form, of all the practices covered in this manual.

Complementary

A final note before you dive in. This manual is full of yoga practices, some more accessible than others. As with any exercise regime, please consult with your physician to see if these practices are right for you. Nothing in this book is meant to take the place of current treatments or medications. This work is complementary, full of tools meant to support what was is already working for you. Share this book with your medical professionals, bodyworkers, and mental health providers, involve them in what you are doing for your wellness!

Enjoy!

FILLING YOUR CUP:
ESTABLISHING THE SACRED CONTAINER

When I first started teaching yoga, I said yes to every substitute request and every teaching gig that came my way. When I was subbing at The Providence Institute, where I got my certification, they would sometimes call me an hour before they needed a sub (I lived a mile away). I might teach a 7am, 9am, 12pm, 5pm, and a 6:30pm in a day. I drove all over the place to teach yoga classes, sometimes as much as an hour in each direction. I made $20 - $30 per class. That does not seem bad, but when you figure in that I might have to drive an hour in each direction to teach an hour-long class, that meant I was make $6 - $10 an hour. It was rough.

I also might not teach any classes in a day. To make ends meet, I had all kinds of odd jobs. I did administrative work for Amy (I could not believe my teacher had me helping her!), housesitting, administrative work for other people, organizational work for people at their homes because I am good at that, and in one odd case, I even did a product reset at several grocery stores (which meant moving products around on a shelf).

Some mornings I would wake up before the sun at someone else's house and drive to teach an early morning class. Then I would drive to someone else's house for work. Then on to Amy's house, maybe another class, my house to be with my boyfriend and dog, and finally back to where I was housesitting. I would manage to eat something in the middle of my day, but it was often something grabbed on the go.

I was exhausted and something had to give. Because I was devoted to what I felt was my calling, it was not going to be the yoga. But it was the yoga in the form of a nourishing personal practice. To support the amount of work and teaching I was doing, I needed to be engaged in a regular practice and I was not. I did not have the time, nor money, to give myself the care that I needed. There were injuries that might have been prevented and illnesses. Had I been smarter in understanding my limitations and how I needed to be making more money per hour, I might have spent my free time seeking out more high paying jobs. As the saying goes, hindsight is 20/20. I am sure that my teaching suffered because of my over extension. In the end, I stopped housesitting and as Amy needed more help because LifeForce Yoga was growing, I was able to back away from doing odds and ends for other people.

This is the high cost of living in a society that does not value what you do – yoga teacher, massage therapists, social workers, schoolteachers, wait staff, and anyone in the service industry. People work themselves to the bone to make ends meet, while serving others, and putting themselves last. You can only put yourself last for so long before it catches up with you.

Self-Inquiry Questions/Writing Prompts:

List three ways (or more) that you take care of yourself:
1.
2.
3.

List three ways (or more) that you take care of others:
1.
2.
3.

Did you struggle in listing the ways you take care of yourself?

Did you find that the list of how you take care of other people was longer?

Empty Cup Syndrome

If you found that your list of caring for others was longer than your list of self-care, then you might be suffering from an Empty Cup Syndrome. Imagine for a moment that you have been gifted a cup to hold all your energy. Each morning you have the opportunity to begin your day with a full cup. If you replenish your cup during the day, you will end the day with a full cup, ready to start the following day. If you do not replenish, you run the risk of ending the day with an empty cup and starting the next day with a cup that is less than half full.

If you are like most people, at one point you had a full cup of energy. You started giving to others, sharing your time, putting others ahead of you, all with the best intentions. There were times you filled your cup after it became empty. As you took on more responsibilities, you had less time to fill your cup. Instead of taking time to build your energy, you fuel yourself with caffeine, sugar, chocolate, food, or anything else that seems to work. To help yourself unwind each night, you need supported relaxation in form of TV, Netflix, wine, and maybe sleep aids. Responsibilities taken on with love and desire begin to feel like burdens and you find yourself dreaming of running away.

YOU ARE NOT ALONE!

What would happen if you took some time for yourself each day? Imagine how you would feel if you spent some time each morning to recharge and reenergize with some simple practices. Imagine how you would feel if you spent time at the end of your day to unwind with some simple practices. It is easy to that there isn't enough time, you don't have the space in your home, your children come first, and/or you don't want to get up earlier.

1. Yes, you do have the time. It is about prioritizing yourself and reallocating time spent elsewhere.
2. You don't need extra space in your home to do LifeForce Yoga practices.
3. Imagine the success and confidence it would build in your children if you taught them the importance of taking care of themselves.
4. Start with five minutes. Think of it as a microdose of yoga. Start with a practice in your bed. Small and simple steps towards a goal ensures success.

How do you recharge?

When you fill your cup, you feel energized, clear, focused, calm, and grounded. When challenges arise, you meet them with head on and with some clarity. The good news is that you already know what helps you recharge; the trick is committing to the daily practice of those tools. Below is a simple list of tools and practices to help you fill your cup. As you look over this list, let yourself be inspired to create some time to practice something from this list.

- Yoga breathing
- Yoga practice
- Meditation
- Exercise
- Walking
- Nature / forest bathing
- Earthing
- Silence
- A hot bath
- Massage
- Essential oils

You will learn new breathing practices, yoga techniques, and meditations that support you in filling your cup as you read this book.

Experience: Recharge

Create a list of things that help you feel calm, clear, focused, grounded, and ready to meet your day. Think outside the box – draw pictures, add colors, paste in magazine pictures, etc. Think of this as Vision Board for recharging. Come back to this page every time you need a little support or when you encounter something you would like to add to this list.

The Sacred Container

The work of LifeForce Yoga and awakening your Inner Radiance begins with the sacred container. Think of your container as a place, real or energetic, where you feel comfortable exploring techniques, body movements, energy, feelings, thoughts, and beliefs. This container should also feel secure, free from disturbances when you are in your practice. We call this container sacred because reconnecting with your Divine essence is no small thing!

Start with creating a physical space in your home. If you have an extra room where you can close a door, this is perfect. If you do not have extra space, think about setting aside a corner of your home. This corner is where you can keep a cushion, a blanket, a journal, inspirational objects, a yoga mat, and even create an altar. Your altar is a special place to fill with objects that soothe and remind you of your wholeness, like pictures, images, icons, religious items, etc. An altar does not have to be religious, nor are you praying to the objects on it. Your altar is representative of your sacred space and the ways in which you devote your energy. I have a love altar that is filled with gifts given in love, hearts, and images of my husband and our marriage. It is a reminder of my commitments and where I turn my gaze when I need a little extra love in my life.

Your sacred container is more than a physical location in which to practice reconnecting. It is also an energetic container. You might think of this as your aura and/or your boundaries. This is the part of your sacred space that you always carry with you. The more you connect to this container, the stronger it will feel, and the easier it will be to settle into this space in different locations.

When you work with others, you create a sacred container, even though you might not think about it. You place images around you that help you feel comfortable while serving others. You use lighting and sounds that support the work you do with others. Parents create and decorate their children's rooms to in a soothing and calming manner that also supports learning. A massage therapist creates a warm atmosphere with soothing lighting, calming scents, and relaxing music. A mental health professional has soothing images in their office, with adequate lighting, a comfortable place to sit, and provides tissues. School teachers, parents, doctors, dentists, hotel managers, restaurateurs, business owners, anyone within the service industry is thinking about the space within which they provide their services. They are looking to create an atmosphere that patrons find nourishing. Why should your home space for practice be any different?

Using the Five Elements in Your Sacred Space

You are an elemental being. Within you there are the five elements that make up the world: Earth, Water, Fire, Air, and Space. Connecting to these elements supports grounding into the present moment, your being, and your Inner Radiance. There is much to be said about the elements. For our purposes, let's look at the elements in relation to our sacred container and space.

Earth is solid, strong, fortified, enduring, and nourishing. Start simple with a landscape image, maybe of your favorite tree, or a place in nature that you wish to visit. A simple physical representation might be sand or dirt. You might choose a more solid form of Earth, like a crystal or rock. If you are needing stronger boundaries in life, use a stone like black tourmaline, red jasper, or hematite. The energy in these stones is more grounding, protective and securing. You can place flowers in your altar space each week. Maybe a plant feels more appropriate for you; one that is planted in dirt. Perhaps you would like a plant that clears constrictive energy, like a spider plant or an ivy. Aloe and cacti are said to absorb electromagnetic frequencies (EMFs) and other energies. The spines on a cactus certainly send a message.

Water is soft, fluid, creative, feeling, and nourishing. Building on the image for the earth element, maybe your image also contains the ocean. Maybe you like mermaids, fish, sharks, dolphins, or whales. A little difficult to put one of those on your altar but there are plenty of images to use. Try an essential oil diffuser, a waterfall, or simply a bowl of water. A flower in a vase brings in both Earth and Water in one object while brightening our space and lifting our moods. A seashell is a reminder of the spiral of life and the ocean. I personally like to use a space clearing spritzer with Palo Santo, Sage, Frankincense, Rosemary, and several other oils. As I sit down in my space, I like to spray my altar, myself, and the area around me. This is a great alternative to incense, especially when you travel.

Fire is hot, intense, cleansing, and transformative. Maybe your nature image includes the shining sun. Place a tea light on your altar. If you want to get more complicated, you can learn how to use a butter lamp, which provides a nice warm light. You could also use a larger candle with a color that has meaning and that is scented. Incense is a nice option. If that is too much, open your space to the light of the sun. Bringing in the fire element connects us to our internal light and can represent the flame of your Inner Radiance You do not want to leave a candle going unattended in your home, so blow it out when you are finished with your practices.

Air is mobile, cool, movement, and light. An image of the clouds in the sky brings in the lightness and movement of air. A feather is representative of the air element. Rather than purchase a feather, or pluck one off a bird, you may have a feather that you found on the ground that has meaning to you. Not into feathers? Try windchimes or even a wind instrument, like a flute, or an ocarina. Perhaps you have a decorative fan that you would like to display on your altar. Even more simple, add some windblown seeds.

Space, or ether, is the most subtle of the elements and is traditional to Ayurveda (Indian Medicine) and Eastern Philosophy. It is called *akasha*. Space is eternal, all-pervading, light, and subtle. It is unlimited potential and possibility. Ether is the space in which all things arise. Bringing space into your sacred space is literally the space between things. As you build your altar, it means making sure that you are not cluttering the space with too many objects.

Experience: Create Your Sacred Space

What do you need for your personal sacred space? Think about the lighting, the temperature, and even sounds in this place. Review your list of things that recharge you and add reminders. For instance, if you listed nature as something that fills your cup, maybe you can place your sacred space in front of a window facing the outdoors. If that is not possible, add a picture to your wall of your favorite place in nature. Get creative with how you decorate your sacred space, so that it nourishes you when you step into it.

Creating the Sacred Container in LifeForce Yoga

Now that you have your own sacred space, or at least the idea of your sacred space in your home and/or workspace, let's explore the sacred space in LifeForce Yoga. We start by connecting to three different concepts. I will use some archetypes as we move through this discussion because the imagery and/or stories behind them work best to convey these concepts. There may be other images that work better for you, if so, feel free to replace the suggested images with your own.

The Elephant

Long before there were bulldozers and other machinery, people used what was available to clear the space. In India, the bulldozer was, and in some cases, still is an elephant. When one needed to clear a path through the jungle, an elephant could uproot trees to make a path. The elephant is strong, stable, and enduring. They have long lives and build strong connections to each other and humans. Inviting the energy of the elephant to helps to clear internal and external space. Invite this energy to support you and to cultivate endurance. The journey of transformation is not short, nor is it easy. You may need the elephant to clear the blocks that constrict your Inner Radiance.

Ganesha, a deity within Hinduism, has the head of an elephant on a human body. He is known as "the remover of obstacles," who also brings up obstacles to be removed. This image is a marriage of our human nature with that of the elephant energy – focused, amiable, and enduring. If this image calls to you, connect with it.

Ring of Fire

We look to Shiva, depicted in as Nataraja, the fire dancer. In the context of LifeForce Yoga, the fire dancer represents two aspects: commitment and staying present. The commitment you make is to do something different. You identify the patterns that are not serving you in the way they once were and that you need something different. Shiva stands in the ring of fire and is committed to be there until he is done. In yoga, we call this *tapas*, the burning desire to make a change.

This image symbolizes the strength and the commitment to stay present to all that arises without numbing out. Yes, sometimes numbing out is an important self-care strategy. Numbing out, or escapism, in not inherently bad or good, it just is. As long as you come back to what you need a time out from, numbing out will not become a constriction. For growth and change, you need to feel our feelings and allow them to move through you. This is self-study, or self-inquiry. You will find many self-inquiry questions throughout this book. In yoga, we call this *svādyāya*, which means to really know and understand ourselves.

In the yogic texts, you will see *svādyāya* also defined as "study of the scriptures." For a long time, I wondered why this was. I did not understand the relationship between studying myself and studying an ancient text like the Yoga Sūtras of Patañjali. One day I was reading a text called Vasistha's Yoga. In this text, Rama is struggling with life and his purpose. In his suffering, he was asking questions about the purpose of life. In that moment, I saw myself reflected and understood my own suffering as a teenager better. I had asked the same questions, without receiving an answer. In the next moment, I had a visceral knowing myself as a divine being. If we are created in the image of God, then to study scripture is to study ourselves.

Taken together, commitment and self-study are the practice of self-awareness. The practice of yoga is the pathway to self-realization. It is releasing the constrictions of doubt, shame, labels, and illusions to understand yourself as whole. You know yourself as the light of Divine energy, your Inner Radiance.

Compassionate Embrace

How long could you dance in the fire of commitment and self-awareness without burning up or burning out? A rhetorical question with very real consequences. You need support. This is where you invite a compassionate embrace. Kwan Yin, or Avalokiteshvara, from the Buddhist tradition is compassion. The name literally translates to, "she/he who hears the cries of the world's suffering." Depicted in Tibetan Buddhism, Avalokiteshvara has

1,000 arms, which represent the 1,000 forms that Kwan Yin/Avalokiteshvara takes to support and help us when we falter. Mother Mary from the Christian tradition is another beautiful example of this supportive embrace.

In yoga, the compassionate embrace is called *īśvarapranidāna*, which means "surrender" and "welcoming the gifts and grace of the Divine into your life." If it resonates, you might also think of this as "letting go and letting God." You commit to your practice, doing something different, and staying present. This is hard work and to complete it you ask for assistance and support. Yoga teaches us that you are not separate, which means that we are all in this together.

You are this compassionate embrace for those that you serve. The parent is this energy for their children. The professional is this energy for clients and students. Learning how to hold yourself in the light of compassion, you need(ed) someone to teach you how. The Yoga Teacher, the Teacher, the Mental Health Professional teach their students and clients all about compassion by being present, listening, creating the sacred container, and the myriad of other ways they express support. Make sure that you are offering yourself this compassion and support!

Tapas svadyaya isvarapranidanani kriya yoga

"Commitment, self-study, and surrender are the yoga that clears the space for the reunification with your Inner Radiance." Put another way, self-awareness with compassion is the practice of yoga. This is the first sūtra (aphorism) from the second chapter of Patanjali's Yoga Sūtras. This text was written down in 400 CE and is understood to be much older. The Yoga Sūtras provide a framework for understanding yourself, a guide for mental health and wellness, and a pathway for freedom from suffering. My teacher Rama Jyoti Vernon calls this text the Gateway to Enlightenment. The sūtras will pop up quite a bit throughout these pages.

Centering

Let's combine all the wisdom and tools into one technique, the centering practice. Centering means to come back to yourself and to come to the present. Centering helps you to establish a connection to yourself, and others, and allows you to arrive in the here and now. It is a process of allowing the outer world and distractions to fall away so that you can focus on your internal world. In a session, leading students or clients through a centering brings everyone to the same page.

Centering strategies take all shapes and sizes. Sometimes it is lighting a candle and pausing. Other times it might be sitting in silence for five minutes. These are valid strategies. When you suffer from anxious thoughts, a racing mind, ruminating over an incident, or fearful thoughts, sitting in silence is not the most effective strategy for coming to the present moment. Instead you might spend that time thinking your anxious thoughts or ruminating. Those five minutes of silence might make you more uncomfortable and even increase your suffering. You might sit silently for five minutes because the teacher asked you, and you want to please them. If you are new to the practice, you might not want to come back because you were uncomfortable.

In LifeForce Yoga, we use a centering strategy with many tools and practices to anchor the mind in the present moment. A centering includes:

- Body awareness
- Breath awareness
- Guided breathing
- Sound
- Intention setting

A centering might also include:

- Hand gestures
- Connecting with an energy or an attitude

By the time you finish this book, you will know all seven of these techniques. For now, you can use the following centering strategy. You may even want to record yourself leading it and practice with the recording.

Experience: Centering

A centering strategy does not have to be this long or extensive. This is an example of the centering that we do during our training programs and weekend retreats. We start our programs this way to connect with each other and allow people to create that sacred space for themselves.

Come into a seated position and become comfortable. If you are seated on the floor, use a cushion to support your hips. Bring the shoulders up to the ears and sigh the breath out as you release the shoulders. Allow the eyes to soften. Begin to greet your body in this moment. Notice areas of tension or tightness. Notice areas of openness or relaxation. Become aware of the ways in which your body is speaking to you in this moment without trying to fix or change anything. Sense into your breath. Notice where you feel the most movement of breath and where you feel the least movement of breath. Again, not trying to fix or change anything. Welcome the breath.

Begin to imagine the breath moving in and out of the brow point at the center of the forehead. You might even feel the movement of the breath. If you wish, image that a candle flame is flickering at the brow point; feeling its warmth if a visualization is not accessible to you. As you breathe, this candle flame is illuminating the seeds of clarity. Illuminating seeds of intuition. Illuminating seeds of wisdom and inner knowing. This is the light of self-awareness. As you inhale, let the light of self-awareness become stronger. As you exhale, release blocks to self-awareness, to inner knowing. Taking two more breaths here.

Let's enhance this light of self-awareness and dissolve the fog of unknowing by using the seed sound for the brow point, the tone of Om. Allow this sound to be low, piercing through the clouds that obstruct your clear sight, like a foghorn, guiding you with clarity and ease to your inner wisdom. Exhale all the breath. Inhale and on the next exhale use the sound of "Om."

Continue to breathe and bring this candle flame down to the heart center. Perhaps imagining the breath moving in and out through the heart. Maybe imagining or feeling this candle flame at the heart center. As you breathe, this candle flame is illuminating the seeds of self-care. Illuminating the seeds of self-compassion. Illuminating the seeds of self-forgiveness and love. This is the light of self-acceptance. As you inhale, allow the light of compassion to grow. As you exhale, releasing whatever blocks the fullest expression of compassion within you. Taking two more breaths here.

Let's enhance this light of self-acceptance by using the seed sound for the heart center, the tone of "yam," with an emphasis on the y-sound. Allow this tone to be low, like that foghorn, piercing through the fog that obstructs your truest self-acceptance. Exhale all the breath. Inhale d on the next exhale use the sound of "yam."

Now let's bring the lights of self-awareness and self-acceptance together in the true heart, which lies beyond constriction and unknowing. This is the hridaya. Bring the left hand to the center of the chest and right hand on top. Feel the breath moving under the hands. Perhaps feeling the heart beating under the hands. Let's connect with this heart that loves unconditionally and for no reason at all, using its seed sound, the tone of "hreem." We'll use this sound three times on three exhales to invoke the depths of love, compassion, self-awareness, and self-acceptance. Exhale all the breath. Inhale for sound… "hreem, hreem, hreem." Inhale… "hreem, hreem, hreem." One more time, vibrating the heart… "hreem, hreem, hreem."

In the silence that remains, allow the sound to reverberate in the space of the true heart. Perhaps feeling more connected to this essence of love and self-acceptance, your Inner Radiance. In this connection, invite a prayer to arise. Your heart is offering up prayers for growth and well-being all day. Allow one of these prayers, these seeds, to surface. If it seems as though the heart is silent, really it is offering you seeds of stillness and openness. Welcome whatever prayer your heart is offering. Nourish it with the breath and your attention. Let's use the sound of Om to vibrate and call this prayer forth into being. Exhale all the breath. Inhale for "Om."

Now, let's offer up another Om, to honor our connections to each other, to acknowledge the support we receive from others. Exhale all the breath. Inhale for "Om."

This time, as we offer up our Om, let's do so in service to everyone around us, who is on their journey through change, growth, and this life. As we offer this third Om, allow the arms to float open in front of you as though you are offering the gifts of love, compassion, and acceptance. Exhale all the breath. Inhale for "Om."

Allow the hands to release down to the lap, resting the aftereffects of your Oms. Noticing if you feel more connected to your heart. Inhale and bring hands together in front of you, interlacing the fingers, crossing the right thumb over the left. Extend the index fingers, allowing them to touch along their length. This is Kali Mudrā. On your next inhale bring Kali Mudrā over the head as you straighten the arms. If you have shoulder issues, feel free to hold this mudrā in front of the heart. Exhale here. If you wish, tilt the chin down, inhale and retain the breath. Otherwise keep breathing. We'll be using the sound of "Ng" to vibrate the crown of the head, while we lower the arms

out to our sides and down to the earth. If you have exhaled, inhale here… "ng." Again, bring the arms into Kali Mudrā as you inhale. Retain the breath if you wish. This time as we lower the arms, imagine that you are cleansing the space around you with breath and sound, creating a sacred container around. If you have exhaled, inhale… "Ng."

Allow the hands to rest, the body to rest. Feel yourself within the container of your own energy. Feel how the legs and hips receive the support of the Earth beneath them. Notice the palms of the hands, warm or cool. Maybe you feel energy awake in the hands and the arms. Become aware of how the breath is moving in the body, the rise and fall of the abdomen or the rib cage. Sense into the heart space again and that seed that your heart offered up. Affirming it once more. When you are ready, allow the eyes to blink open slowly and to find the horizon.

Self-inquiry questions/writing prompt:
- How did it feel to use sound?
- Did you feel vibration in the brow point and/or the heart?
- Did a prayer arise from the heart?
- What did you feel in your body after this centering was complete?
- How do you feel after this practice?

Summary

In a world where exhaustion and being busy seems like a badge of courage, create the opposite for yourself. Living life with a full cup allows you to enjoy all that life has to offer you. Start with identifying the things that work to support you in replenishing and rejuvenating your energy. Next create a sacred space for filling your cup and reconnecting to your Inner Radiance. Practice a centering strategy each time you come to your sacred space. You can use the script above or whatever abbreviated form of it you would like.

ENERGY FLOWS WHERE THE MIND GOES:
SPIRITUAL INTENTION

When I started yoga, it was simply to feel better. I was suffering and I no longer wanted to feel that way. At the beginning of each session, Amy Weintraub would invite us to welcome the "heart's deepest longing, the burning bush in your heart." I was always able to connect with something – peace, healing, focus, relaxation, strength, abundance, etc. Sometimes I was altruistic, other times it was all about me. Intention gave the practice meaning, it helped me to see why I was there. These intentions made my practice a sacred engagement, instead of a simple exercise class.

Then I took the LifeForce Yoga Practitioner training. We did a practice to clear some space and invite a *sankalpa*, a spiritual intention/heartfelt prayer. Over the years of assisting the training, I had many options to partake in this practice. Each time a sankalpa arose for me and they were all different. I felt connected to each of these sankalpas. They felt true and authentic. And they were always different.

I wanted to understand more about sankalpa and decided to do more research. I came across a piece where several yogis were interviewed about sankalpa. They said that the sankalpa came from the deepest recesses of the heart and only appeared when the practitioner had cleared enough space to receive this gift from the heart. Once the sankalpa arrived it never changed. Ooo, I was intrigued. I understood why my sankalpa changed like the seasons. It was an intention, not really my heart's deepest wish for me.

At this time, I had just started a Navratri (a Hindu festival to honor the Goddess) practice with Shiva Rea. We were invited to set an intention for the nine days. I decided to pick a sankalpa and that I would stay with it, without changing it, for a year. I wrote it down and affirmed it with every practice and class I taught. I felt very clear that this was an intention picked with my heart in mind and my reasoning was to focus my energy so that it would come true.

Six months later, we were at Sivananda Ashram in The Bahamas leading our annual LifeForce Yoga program there. I went to the morning and evening satsangs (gatherings for meditation, chanting, and teachings), making sure that I arrived for meditation each session. There I would affirm my sankalpa. One evening, I was focused on my heart. I was imagining my breath at the heart and repeating a mantra at my heart. All of a sudden, my heart spoke to me. "Love, just love," it said. My eyes flew open and I felt like I had been hit by a ton of energetic bricks. It was undeniable, from its depths, my heart had given me my sankalpa. After six months of dedication to the process, I had arrived at my sankalpa. The journey to get there had taken over a decade.

Months later, I was having an issue with someone. I do not remember the issue, nor do I remember the person. All I remember is that I was frustrated. In my mind, I was running over the different things I was going to say to this person, as one does when they are upset. I went stomping into my bedroom to retrieve a book, completely focused on how to "put this person in their place." As I bent over to pick up my book, my heart and mind offered up my sankalpa. I froze in place, in awe, because all my frustration had dissolved. I was reminded of what was most important to my growth and well-being. This concocted situation and expenditure of energy was not of significance. There was no letting go of feelings, or clearing things away, it was all gone, in an instant. It was in this moment that I truly understood the power of a sankalpa.

Over the years, when confronted with an issue, I connect with my heart felt prayer. It is the yard stick against which everything is measured. Is this important? Does this deserve my energy? When my reactions dissolve in the face of my sankalpa, I move on. When my feelings, emotions, and beliefs remain in the presence of my sankalpa, I know that I need to pursue a response.

What is Your Why?

Now that the container is in place it is time to connect with your Why. What is the reason that you have chosen to walk down this path? Why are you engaged in transformation? Where do you want to go? Your reason for cracking this book to change your life is because you want to feel different than you do right now. Let us start the process to discovering the deeper reasons and longings for making these changes.

Intention

An intention is defined as an aim or a plan. We use them all the time. We intend to clean the house later, call a friend, go to the store, get an early start, etc. Yoga teachers set them in classes and workshops for hip opening, kindness, rest, etc. In yoga, an intention is a desired outcome that you would like as a result of your practice. It is where you want to focus your energy, how you want to feel by the end of the practice, or something that you hope to gain. Intentions are practical and often an immediate focus.

Intentions are set in the present and positive tense. They are set in the present tense to establish a greater connection with it happening right now. The future never arrives, it is always right now. We affirm it in the present moment, as though it is happening, to create the thought, belief, and energy flow to the now. Intentions are set in the positive tense because the mind does not fully understand negations. When we say, "I am less stressed," the mind does not comprehend less of something, so it hears "I am stressed." The very thing we are trying to release is affirmed in the present moment. If we want to be less stressed, then the thing we need to connect with is what it would look and feel like if we had no stress. That might be peaceful, relaxed, at ease, balanced, calm, focused, on vacation, at the beach, camping, hanging out with friends, etc. The opposite to stressed out is personal because we all experience stress relief in different ways.

Sankalpa

The Sanskrit word "sankalpa" is translated as intention. *San* means "to become one with," and *kalpa* means "time" and "subconscious mind." In LifeForce Yoga, we invoke sankalpa as your Heartfelt Prayer, or your Spiritual Intention. It is the foundation for spiritual growth and well-being. The sankalpa is how the heart shares and reminds us of our innate wholeness and Inner Radiance. Sankalpa is the link between our yoga practice and our lives. It inspires our daily practice.

We are spiritual beings living in human form, often distracted by shiny objects. We get caught up in striving towards things, belongings, and money. Society, advertising, and habit tell us that ease and completion come from owning stuff. After a time, we find that the things we own are not bringing us the ease, peace, or love, that we have been seeking. We can buy more stuff, or we can try something different. This is when we turn our attention to the spirit, the soul, or whatever you might call that part of you that is more than this body. Spiritual Fulfillment is being aware and living from a place of deep connection to your Inner Radiance. Your Spiritual Intention is the light that guides you to and reminds you that you are already whole.

The sankalpa is invited after connecting with the heart. When we clear enough space, the sankalpa reveals itself to us. For some, this happens immediately, and for others, this takes time. The high cost of living is that heart gets constricted. We all experience this. When there are many constrictions around the heart, it can be difficult to hear what it is saying to you. This is why we practice connecting with and clearing space around the heart. The sankalpa is the nectar of yoga. If you don't have one, you will eventually. Give yourself patience and time to receive your sankalpa. Remember, it took more than 10 years for my sankalpa to reveal itself to me! With these tips and practices, you may receive one sooner.

Experience: Discovering Spiritual Fulfillment

Find a comfortable position for an imagination practice. You may wish to lie down or maybe find a seated meditation position. Feel how the body is supported by the earth. Feel how the body breathes itself in and out. Take three deep full breaths here. With each exhale, invite distractions to release. Take a deep breath in and hold the breath at the top, squeeze as many muscles as you can, making fists and scrunching up the face. With a big sigh, let it go. Release. Do that again. Taking a deep breath in, hold the breath at the top, and scrunch up the face, the fingers, the arms, the toes, the glutes, as many muscles as possible. Use a big sigh to let it go. One more time, make it count. Deep breath in and scrunch up everything, hold the breath, squeeze, squeeze, squeeze, squeeze, squeeze, squeeze, squeeze, squeeze, and sigh it out. Completely releasing any tensions.

Let the breath return to its natural rhythm, perhaps feeling a little more ease of breath, or a little more softness or relaxation in the body. Begin to imagine yourself fulfilled on a spiritual level. What does that feel like for you? Where do you feel spiritual fulfillment in your own body? Become totally absorbed in imagining that you are spiritually fulfilled. Notice where the attention is drawn within the body. Is there a relaxation present? A sense of ease? A softness? How does the body breathe when you are spiritually fulfilled? Imagine this spiritual fulfillment. Where is the breath in the body? How does the breath flow? Is it long or short? Notice the speed of the breath. Perhaps colors or images arise. Welcome whatever is present.

As you imagine yourself in this place of spiritual fulfillment. What are you doing? Where are you in the world when you are spiritually fulfilled? Or does that even matter? There may even be beings present that support you on your journey of spiritual fulfillment. Who are those beings? Let yourself dive fully into this experience. Remain fully present to your experience of your spiritual fulfillment. Keep breathing with your experience of your spiritual fulfillment.

You might even ask yourself how did I get here? How did I arrive in my spiritual fulfillment? Welcome the response. Let go of any self-editing. Even the urge to say no that's not right, that is not possible.

Receive this wisdom from yourself and feel free to stay here as long as you need, communing with the you that is spiritually fulfilled. Whenever you are ready deepen your breath begin to move the body.

Write down anything about this experience that you wish to record.

Self-Inquiry Questions/Writing Prompts:

Continuing the discovery of the spiritual intention, let's explore some questions that may shine light on what your spiritual intention is. As you answer these self-inquiry questions, do so without thinking about the answer. You can create a list, write in complete sentences, draw pictures, whatever works for you. If you are able, you may wish to write with your non-dominant hand. Use your journal or the space below.

- This is what expands me:

- When I feel most like myself, I am engaged in these activities:

- This is what wholeness looks and feels like to me:

- I feel that my purpose is:

- This is what my spirit/heart is longing for:

Now that you have finished your writing, go back over your list. Circle all the items that are the juiciest, the most meaningful, or that seem to jump of the page. Because a spiritual intention is about you and your personal growth, circle the things that are all about you. From here, what is most important to you on this list?

Formulating Your Spiritual Intention

All things start as a seed. Your writing exercise gave you many seeds to plant. Now it is for you to decide which seed you want to nourish and grow. The Spiritual Intention, or sankalpa, is the seed that when nourished guides you through life, that helps you make important decisions, and that reminds you of what is most important to you. Let's turn this seed into an affirmation, mantra, or prayer.

Once you have found your intention, creating an affirmation statements helps to connect with this intention. You can write it on a piece of paper in your office space, use it as a screen saver, leave yourself sankalpa notes, or get even more creative. Here are some guidelines:
- Make sure the affirmation is short enough that you can remember it.
- Present tense – this is something that you are bringing into the now.
- Positive tense – this is a seed that you are growing, something that you want to increase.

- Include I-statements that make your affirmation more real to you, like "I am," or "I have," or "I welcome," or "---breathes through me now."
- Use your intuition, you know what works best for you.

An example:

Let's say you would like to be less stressed out. What is the opposite of stressed out, or what would it look like if you were less stressed? A couple of examples of the opposite: peaceful, easeful, relaxed, calm, tranquil, etc. Now bring it into the present moment, following our guidelines. For instance, "I am peaceful," or "relaxation breathes through me now," or as Amy Weintraub says, "I am open and available to receive tranquility."

The last piece, that is really important, is to anchor your intention. This can be done by cultivating visualization, an experience, a memory, or a feeling in the body. Not everyone feels comfortable with creating visual images, so using a feeling in the body is an excellent alternative, otherwise known as a "felt sense." It may be a visualization of yourself achieving your intention; down to the precise detail (what you are wearing, where you are). It may be an image that represents your intention. It could also be the feeling in the body when your intention is achieved.

Using the example above, you might imagine your shoulders softening. Or yourself resting peacefully in a relaxation pose in a yoga class. It might be a feeling of taking very deep breaths. It might be an image of your favorite beach. Whatever you choose, make sure that if feels authentic to you. Now that you have a sankalpa to work with, you can use the Bhāvanā practice instill it at a deeper level.

> "This subtle force of repeated suggestion overcomes our reason. It acts directly on our emotions and our feelings, and finally penetrates to the depths of our subconscious minds. It's the repeated suggestion that makes you believe." – Claude Bristol

Summary

Connecting with a Spiritual Intention helps to guide and inspire practice. In the beginning, we create a sankalpa, picking something that we feel connected to or want to create. As we continue to practice and clear space our heart begins to speak and a sankalpa is revealed to us. We can understand this offering from the heart to be a spiritual calling and guide for our life.

I GOT A NEW ATTITUDE
BHĀVANĀ

Vitarka badhane pratipaksha bhāvanām
Where there are constricting cognitions or feelings, cultivate the opposite.
– Yoga Sutras of Patanjali, 1:33

I was 17 and at summer camp in North Carolina, lying down for a nap. I started to experience a sense of things dissolving and I could not feel where I ended and everything else began. It was a strange and uncomfortable experience. I brushed it off.

After I got home, it started happening, every day in the afternoon. It was like I was experiencing the entirety of the universe, of existence, all at the same time. I saw myself as an insignificant speck on a blue ball floating in space. In many ways, it was like the truth of reality was exposed to me. I was terrified. I began to wonder what the point of going to high school was, of getting a job, or doing anything. I served no purpose and I was just going to die. Why bother with any of this?

The time in between these episodes was filled with nothing. I no longer felt like me, I did not want to participate in anything. I had read The Bell Jar by Sylvia Plath the year before and I understood what she meant about being under the bell jar. Existence was unbearable, and yet, unlike Plath, I felt no need to end my life. Had I not gotten treatment, that might have changed.

I was taken to a therapist, then a psychiatrist, and was diagnosed with panic attacks related to depression. They gave me meds. The episodes stopped, the bell jar disappeared, and I felt normal again.

Prior to seeing the psychiatrist, the therapist gave me a tool that was so powerful that I use it to this day. I remember sitting in her office in a big fluffy chair. She asked me to close my eyes and think of a special place where I felt calm. My mind went to a trip we had taken to Northern California years prior. We had parked the car and walked a short path through trees to get to the beach. The image that arose in my mind was stepping off a forest path,

28

littered with pine needles, to the beach. In my mind, I stop there and look out across the sand. It is cloudy and gray with a light drizzle of rain. Down the curve of the beach there was a mountain rock jutting out. I can see the dark shapes of birds flying above the rock. The beauty of it absorbs me and I feel like I am back there, and everything is at peace.

I described this to my therapist. She had me hold the visualization and I took some deep breaths. She told me that any time I felt a panic attack coming on, I should visualize this experience. It did not heal or stop the panic attacks. It did help me feel supported and calmer during those terrifying hours that I would spend in that state. Today, when I need a break or I feel a little anxious, I go right back to that beach. This is the power of visualization.

Before we dive into Bhavana, I feel it is important to share my thoughts on that experience. After years of self-study, I believe that I was experiencing a spiritual awakening. I have had a couple of panic attacks in the years since and they were always accompanied by an inability to breathe. Those 2-3 hour experiences every day were filled with terror and tears, but I was not struggling to breathe. That sense of boundaries dissolving happens when I am in meditation or feeling deeply connected to source energy. I am also reminded of being a child and getting sick. I would have these experiences of leaving my body to escape the pain and discomfort (what I now know as dissociation). In those times, I felt expansive and radiant, looking down at my body. There was a sense of comfort, the only way to not feel the pain that I was feeling. The difference between now and then is that I have control over the experience, rather than being inflicted with the awesome experience of knowing the Universe as it really is.

What is Bhāvanā?

Bhāvanā is often defined as a visualized goal. It is unknown where this definition or understanding originated, as the word itself means something different. Bhāvanā means "cultivation." *Bhava* means "attitude" and *na* means the "eternal cosmic vibration." Based on this information, a more appropriate understanding of bhāvanā is "cultivating an attitude that brings us closer to the eternal cosmic vibration," which could mean that which you hold dear, or even the energy that sourced you. In other words, cultivating something that brings you closer to the source of your Inner Radiance, beneath the constrictions, wants, needs, and desires.

Bhāvanā is so much more than just a visualization, even though it could include imagery for those that are inclined. In many ways, it is key to the practice of yoga and LifeForce Yoga. For example, when we focus on an intention for a class, we begin to formulate a vision for how that class will occur. When we are in a warrior pose, we are invited to connect with strength; this is bhāvanā. We use it a lot more than we think that we do.

From the understanding of the yoga sutras, the practice of bhāvanā is about reorienting the mind towards growth and wellbeing. From Yoga Sutra 1:33, Patanjali says, "where there are constrictions, cultivate the opposite." We readily identify what is not working for us and what constricts us; we know them intimately. We can get stuck in our constrictions and see no way out. This experience can be a part of any diagnosis, mental health or otherwise. We begin to identify with the diagnosis, unable to see ourselves as more than our constrictions. With bhāvanā, we are replacing the constriction with an idea of its opposite expression that will lead us to freedom. Only you can identify that expression of freedom for you. Note: bhavana is not a fix for depression, anxiety, trauma, or anything else. It is a PART of the healing process, an add-on to enhance what is already working.

Self-Inquiry Question/Writing Prompt:

Think about the ways in which you connect and cultivate different attitudes and moods. List some of the techniques you already have.

Bhāvanā is an attitude to be cultivated and your attitude is how you present your energy to the world. When you go to a job interview, you cultivate a friendly, upbeat, and confident attitude, even though you may not feel like it. If you were to show up another way, you may not get the job. There are many ways that you change your attitude to move in the world. The good news is that when we work with bhavana and LifeForce Yoga, we can shift our energy so that the bhavana is not a mask, rather it becomes authentic. This takes time and practice.

Self-Inquiry Question/Writing Prompt: What is your energetic footprint?

Take some time to think about how your energy impacts others. Are you a person who brightens up a room or brings the energy down? Are you both at different times? If you are not sure, think about some of the people you know and how their energy impact you.

Using Bhāvanā in LifeForce Yoga

The practice of bhāvanā in LifeForce Yoga is integral. We use it often, sometimes as a stand-alone practice and other times as a part of another practice. Bhavana can be used to strengthen sankalpa (spiritual intention), during breathing practices to anchor the awareness, at the beginning of a session/class to focus attention during the class, in yoga postures to connect to the energy of the pose, during meditation and mudra, as part of a guided relaxation practice, and as a part of the Bhāvanā practice, explored in greater depth below.

Identifying the Constriction

Naming what constricts you can help you to release the grip of that constriction. Think of it as pinpointing yourself on a map. To get to a specific destination, you need to know your starting point. Otherwise, you will wander without direction and the practices will be less effective.

Self-Inquiry Question/Writing Prompt: What constricts me?

Create a list of the things that constrict you, that keep you from expressing your true self. These can be small or big. This does not need to be a comprehensive list.

Identifying the Opposite

When we cultivate an opposite in LifeForce Yoga, we are cultivating an attitude. Some systems focus on an internal visualization that is given by the teacher. In a style where we are focused on empowerment, we want to give people as much agency as possible. Therefore, we focus on the cultivation of an attitude and allowing ourselves to find our own way and connection to this attitude.

The opposite is strongest when it is a sensorial experience. Your bhāvanā could come in the form of a feeling, image, thought, memory, emotion, sound, word, taste, or an inner knowing. The sensorial experience helps you connect to the attitude that you are working to enhance. This connection is authentic because it comes from you. For example, how do you connect with strength? I could give you an image, but if you are not visual the practice will not work for you.

Self-Inquiry Question/Writing Prompt: What Elevates You?

Create a list of the things that expand you, that help you feel more connected, lighter, and brighter. This experience could be physical, energetic, emotional, or mental.

A Special Note on Imagery

Visualization is a tried and true practice that we mastered as children. Every time we played, we exercised our imaginations to enhance whatever game we were playing, be it cops and robbers, dolls, or space exploration. We may have had props, but we built a world for those toys, or ourselves, to inhabit in your mind. There is a lot to be said about the efficacy of visualization on outcomes.

What about people who cannot visualize? Sometimes, when we experience a trauma, we cannot seem to get away from it. The moment keeps coming back to us in our minds. One of the coping mechanisms that we have developed is to lock those stressful and traumatic images up. They get put behind a locked door in our minds. As a result, this can lock away the beneficial images that support and soothe us. When we are invited to find an image, we either cannot, or the door is cracked just a little bit and what we have been trying not to see comes flooding back. If this is you, please know that you do not need to have an image for bhavana to work and trust that when you are ready, you will begin to visualize with ease.

Cultivating Your Opposite

Now that you have identified the constriction, it's time to find the opposite. The best way to find the opposite is to ask yourself, "if I didn't feel this way, how would I feel?" The opposite is the first thing that arises. If you find yourself struggling to find the opposite of a current constriction, check your list of what elevates you. Perhaps there is a specific attitude on that list that seems resonate and that you would like to explore in your life.

This list can support you in finding the opposite:

Abandoned	Connected, Secure, Safe
Aggressive	Assertive
Agitated, Anxious, Nervous, Enraged	Calm, Ease, Peace
Angry	Accepting, Tolerant
Anxious, Apprehensive	Calm, Excited, Joyful, Peaceful, Unafraid
Apathetic, Numb, Disconnected	Connected, Feeling, Love, Present, Responsive
Ashamed, Embarrassed	Confident, Proud
Bashful	Bold
Bored	Interested
Competitive	Cooperative
Confused	Collected, Focused
Cowardly	Courageous, Noble
Dependent	Independent
Depressed	Connected, Elated, Happy, Joyful
Despair, Despondent, Melancholy	Connected, Lighthearted, Loved
Disappointed	Content, Pleased
Discomfort	Comfort
Discontent	Content

Discouraged	Eager, Optimistic
Disgusted	Delighted, Forgiving
Exhausted, Overworked, Tired	Refreshed, Rested
Forgetful	Thoughtful
Frightened	Courageous
Frustrated	Content, Satisfied
Grieving	Loving
Helpless	Courageous, Powerful
Hopeless	Hopeful, Lighthearted
Hysterical	Composed
Insecure	Confident
Insignificant	Important
Intolerant	Thoughtful
Jealous	Trusting
Lethargic	Alert, Awake, Energetic, Present
Lazy, Listless	Energetic, Enthusiastic
Lonely	Connected, Content, Enough
Neglected	Nourished
Numb	Sensitive, Alert, Present, Feeling
Pained	Comfortable
Pressured	Relaxed
Resentful	Accepting, Generous
Sad	Cheerful, Elevated
Scared	Confidant
Separate	Connected
Stressed	Calm, Peaceful, Steady
Tense	Relaxed
Uncertain	Determined, Focused
Uncomfortable	Comfortable
Ungrateful	Grateful
Ungrounded	Grounded
Unhappy	Blissful, Joyful
Unproductive	Creative
Unthinking	Meditative
Violent	Tender
Weak	Powerful, Strong
Worried	Composed

Bhāvanā Practice

In LifeForce Yoga, we also have a special practice that we call Bhavana. This includes the cultivation of the attitude and adds a gesture with sound. The practice is best when done in a seated position, as this makes things easier on the shoulders. The process takes about three to five minutes the first time. Once you are familiar with the practice, the practice may only take a couple of minutes. The basic steps:

1. Cultivate your bhāvanā
2. Inhale the arms up in front of the heart for a count of four
3. Retain the breath as you connect with your bhāvanā (for a count of four)
4. Draw the hands and the bhāvanā to your heart with sound (for a count of six)
5. Repeat four more times
6. Allow the hands to rest on the heart as you breath with your bhāvanā

The sound is important because it helps to stimulate the calm brain response in the nervous system. When we are in this state, we learn better, which in turn helps us to manifest our bhavanas. Let's experience the practice first and then we will explore the relationship between sound, breath, and the nervous system.

Experience: Bhāvanā for Peace

In a seated position, adjust yourself so that the spine is long, and the body is comfortable. Allow the eyes to soften as you connect with an experience of peace. This could be a feeling of peace in the body, an image from nature or your life, maybe the repetition of the word peace in your mind, or any other way that peace comes to you in this moment. If more than one thing has arisen, pick the one that feels most resonant or make a peace collage with all that is arising. Take three breaths to solidify your bhāvanā of peace.

Exhale all the breath. Inhale for a slow count of four. Retain the breath for a count of four as you connect with your bhāvanā for peace. Now exhale slowly to a count of six. Again, inhale for a slow count of four. Retain the breath as you recall your bhāvanā for peace. Exhale with "so-ham," (pronounced so-hummm) drawing it out, so the sound is resonant and soothing. This time inhale the arms up in front of the heart as though you are embracing a ball of peaceful energy. Retain the breath as you connect with your bhāvanā for peace. Exhale with "so-hum" while you draw peacefulness and your hands to your heart. Inhale slowly as you  *bring your arms out in front of the heart. Pause to embrace your bhāvanā for peace. Exhale with "so-hum" as you draw peacefulness and your hands to your heart. Practice two more times.*

Allow the hands to rest on the heart, giving the heart a gentle rock. This bhāvanā for peacefulness is on the altar of your heart. It is available to you, whenever you need to connect with peace. Take two more breaths with the hands resting on the heart. When you are ready, allow the eyes to open.

Self-Inquiry Question/Writing Prompts:

- What is your bhāvanā for peace?

- How do you feel after that practice?

- Do see yourself practicing this when you need more peace?

The preceding example used peace as the bhāvanā. You could use ANY bhāvanā in that practice: energy, calm, confidence, strength, ease, lightheartedness, etc. The sounds we use in the Bhāvanā practice help to cultivate the energy. The practice above uses the mantra and soothing sounds of "so-hum," which means "I am that" to connect with peace. We could also use the soothing sounds of "sha-ma-ya" to connect with peacefulness. The choice is up to personal preference in this case. Sound is an important aspect of LifeForce Yoga and we will dive into mantra and sound in the next chapter. For now, you can use the following list of bhāvanā suggestions and sounds you can combine with them to connect with the desired energy. Add to this list as you develop connections to the sounds and bhāvanās.

Note: the "a" sound below sounds like "ah." When it is followed by an "m," as in "yam," the sound can become more meditative like "yum."

For feelings of depression, or when you need to build your energy	Sound or Mantra
Calm Strength	Ma-ha-ra (draw the hands to the solar plexus) & Ma-ha-ya (draw the hands to the heart)
Energy	Ram
Strength	Dhee-Ree-Ha! or Ram
Uplifting	Yam
Lightheartedness	Yam
Cheer	Yam or So-ham
Hope	Yam or So-ham
Contentment	So-ham
Joyful	Ma-ha-ha!, Yam or So-Ham
Exhilarating	Ram or So-ham
Enthusiasm	Ram, Ma-ha-ha, or So-ham
Vitality	Vam & Ram, Ma-ha-ha, or So-ham
Love	Yam, Hreem, or So-ham
Gratitude	Ma-ha-ya, Yam, or So-ham
Connection	Na-ma-ha, Yam, Om, So-ham, or Sat-yam
Inner Sanctuary	Sha-ma-ya

For feelings of anxiety, or when you need to calm your energy.	Sound or Mantra
Peace	Sha-ma-ya, Shanti, or So-ham
Soothing	Oh-oo-ah-eh-ee-mm-ng, Sha-ma-ya, Shanti, or So-ham
Ease	Oh-oo-ah-eh-ee-mm-ng, Sha-ma-ya, Shanti, or So-ham
Grounding	Lam, Oh & Ooo, or So-ham
Relaxed	Oh-oo-ah-eh-ee-mm-ng, or So-ham
Steady	Lam, or So-ham
Tranquility	Oh-oo-ah-eh-ee-mm-ng, Sha-ma-ya, or So-ham
Calm	Sha-ma-ya, or So-ham
Rest	Oh-oo-ah-eh-ee-mm-ng, Sha-ma-ya, or So-ham
Comfort	Oh-oo-ah-eh-ee-mm-ng, Sha-ma-ya, or So-ham
Soft / Softening	Oh-oo-ah-eh-ee-mm-ng, Sha-ma-ya, or So-ham
Stability	Lam, or So-ham
Love	Yam, Hreem, or So-ham
Gratitude	Ma-ha-ya, Yam, or So-ham
Connection	Na-ma-ha, Yam, Om, So-ham, or Sat-yam
Inner Sanctuary	Sha-ma-ya

Summary

Your energy is how you present yourself to the world. Your energy can get hijacked by your mood. It is possible to change your energy and your mood with the practice of bhāvanā. As the Yoga Sūtras teach, when you feel constricted cultivate the opposite. LifeForce Yoga picks up where the Yoga Sūtras leave off, by giving a practice of connecting with a desired energy, then using sound and movement to instill a connection to this opposite energy. Use this practice as much as you would like.

IF YOU WANT TO SING OUT, SING OUT
THE YOGA OF SOUND

My old friend anxiety is visiting again. There are the normal visitations of anxiety, like anticipation, running late, and even excitement. I am okay with those. But this is intense, gut churning, overwhelming anxiety, that has woken me up in the middle of the night. It is two in the morning and I feel like I am getting ready to have a panic attack. My heart is pounding so loud that I can hear it in my ears. My mind is racing, and I cannot find my breath. I do not want to wake my husband up.

"Stop!!!" I yell in my mind bringing my hand up in front of me. I take a deep breath in and slowly let it out. If it were daytime, I would do some movement, bouncing, or even cleaning. But it is the middle of the night and I need to get some sleep. I start taking slow, deliberate breaths, in and out through my nose. Every inhale I chant "om, śrīm, śrīm, śrīm." Every exhale I chant "om śrīm, śrīm, śrīm." As I chant, I see a matrix of light before and around me. Each repetition strengthens this light and energy.

This mantra is pronounced "shreem" and invites all that is good and supportive, in abundance. It is the mantra of the Hindu goddess Lakshmi. I chant it because it reminds me of my faith that I am being looked after, my devotion to an energy that holds and nurtures me, and my surrender to the will of the Divine essence that is my Inner Radiance. This is a deep and spiritual practice for me. Within minutes, I fall asleep.

My goal in sharing these stories is to be as honest as possible with you. I am not Hindu, nor Christian, nor anything. I fall under the category of Spiritual But Not Religious (SBNR) and I am open to it all. My home was areligious, and I classify my father as an atheist. I remember thinking about God when I was very young and how cruel it would be if we only had one chance to "get things right." I did not know the term reincarnation, but I was thinking about the concept. My doorway into the spiritual came in the form of mantra. I did not know what these beautiful words meant, but I understood them at a cellular level. They bring about a deep peace and ease for me.

The beauty of mantra is that the words create an energetic matrix, a sacred geometry, that focuses my mind on what I am creating. The whole world begins to fall away, and I am reminded of who I really am. From this place of my Inner Radiance, I move forward with ease.

Mantra

The word *mantra* comes from the Sanskrit language, which is the basis for all Indo-European languages including English, Latin, Aramaic, and Arabic. Mantra is composed of two root words, *manas* and *tra*. *Manas* means "the mind" and refers to the reactive, judging, and emotional part of the mind. *Tra* is a little more complex and has numerous translations, like "tool," "to transport," "to protect," or "to set free." When taken together, we understand that mantra is a tool for the mind. The meaning goes beyond intention or a power statement; it is a vehicle to liberate the mind from suffering and to bring us to the realization of our Inner Radiance, that experience of the true self as whole in this moment.

At the beginning of creation, there was a vibration. Many cultures, religions, and belief systems have a name for this vibration. Science calls this vibration The Big Bang. Christianity calls this vibration "the word of G-d." The Vedas (ancient Hindu scriptures) call this vibration "the Divine sound current." Even String Theory is based on vibrating strings of energy that produce particles that make up the world around us. Our underlying reality is a current of unending sound. When we make sacred sound, vocalizations with spiritual intention behind them, we are connecting with the deepest aspects of our being and creation itself.

It is believed that mantra, when said correctly, changes the vibrational fields within our being and aligns those fields with the desired energy. This desired energy, or outcome, is contained within the mantra itself. Mantra is a form of sacred geometry where sound combines with intention to create something new. For example, if we desire enlightenment, we chant The Gāyatrī Mantra. If we desire grounding, chanting Lam increases the Earth Element. Diving deep into the practice of mantra reveals that there are pathways to many desired outcomes. Put simply, a mantra is a mathematical equation that gets one from point A to point B.

A mantra does not have to be religious in nature. The tradition of mantra, in yoga, comes from the religious background of Hinduism. Some of the mantras are secular and some are devotional. In LifeForce Yoga, we use mantras that are non-devotional and help us to connect with an energy, attitude, or an outcome. We use mantras to awaken the elements, to clear the chakras, to prepare for meditation, and to center the mind. We also use sounds to help us connect with a bhāvanā. In other cases, when someone is devout, we might turn to their religion for a prayer that supports the desired outcome.

A mantra, when repeated with an intention helps to focus the mind on that intention. For example, if we are stressed out, we can focus their mind on peacefulness by repeating the word peace, along with a bhāvanā for peace. There is some evidence to suggest that using more ancient languages helps us to get there faster. In this case, chanting the mantra for peace in Sanskrit, which is *shanti* (pronounced shawn-tea), can help create the experience and feeling of peace more effectively than thinking the word peace.

This is not foreign to the human condition. In fact, we do this all the time. When we want something to happen, we think about it, pray for it, and even imagine it happening. When we are driving and we want a green light, we might repeat "green, green, green," in our heads and then it happens. The light was going to turn green anyway (this is an example of correlation, not causation), but think about how this reinforces the behavior in our minds. We engage in this wish for a green light because we might be running late. During the time that we are chanting "green, green, green," the mind is occupied by the image of the green light, not the thought of what is going to happen when we are late. The point is not that we are changing the lights, rather we are focusing the mind on something else.

Basics of the Breath

While mantra gives the mind a focal point, it also helps to control breathing. The breath is both conscious and automatic (or unconscious), meaning we can control it and when we are not thinking about the breath, the body takes care of breathing. The breath is also the reflection of the mind. A fast breath is indicative of an anxious state, a shallow or non-existent breath is indicative of a depressed state. We can also control the mind by changing the breath. We will see many examples of this in coming chapters. For now, let's explore some basic anatomy of the breath.

The lungs are housed in the ribcage. They begin at your collar bones and extend throughout the chest cavity ending at about the base of the breastbone. The lungs are just as complex as the rest of the body, with a surface area that is equivalent to the size of a tennis court. The lungs are attached to the inside of the rib cage by a vacuum. When the chest cavity is punctured, the lung "deflates," or collapses into itself. This vacuum allows the breathing diaphragm to draw air into the lungs and press the air out. There are three lobes to the right lung and two lobes to the left lung, making room for the heart. Oxygen is drawn into the lungs and passes through membranes into the blood stream. Carbon dioxide is released from the cells and exhaled.[1] .

When you take an inhale, the lungs expand in 360 degrees, out to the sides, to the back,

---

[1] The air we inhale is: 78% nitrogen, 21% oxygen, 0.965% argon, 0.04% carbon dioxide, plus helium, water, and other gases. This of course changes depending on location - other molecules may be present in air, like mold, particulates, carbon monoxide, etc.

The air we exhale is: 78% nitrogen, 15-18% oxygen (that's right, you retain very little of it), 4-5% carbon dioxide, 0.96% argon, and trace amounts of metabolites (these are unique to each individual and vary person to person based on your gut biome).

The process of molecules going to and from the cells is called cellular respiration.

to the front, up to the shoulders, and down to the abdomen. The lungs can expand down towards the base of the ribcage. This is why, on an inhale, the abdomen begins to expand, like you have just eaten a large meal. On the exhale, the abdomen moves back toward the spine and the lungs deflate.

The abdominal diaphragm, also known as the breathing diaphragm, or just the diaphragm, is the main muscle of respiration. The diaphragm separates the chest cavity from the abdominal cavity and has openings to allow the esophagus, the psoas muscles, arteries, veins, and nerves to pass through. It looks a little bit like an open umbrella when it is resting. When engaged, it looks like the umbrella is being closed. When the diaphragm engages, it pulls the lungs down, which draws air into your lungs. When you exhale, the diaphragm returns to its resting position underneath the lungs, pressing air out of the lungs. The center of the diaphragm is attached to the pericardium (a double-walled sac around the heart) through connective tissue known as fascia. When you take a deep inhale, the diaphragm gently tugs on your heart. This gentle tug invites the nervous system into a calmer place.

Experience: Breath Experiment

- *Inhale and exhale through the mouth.*
- *Inhale and exhale through the nose. Which breath was longer?*
- *Now, inhale through the nose and exhale through the mouth with the drawn-out sound of "ahh." Which one was longer?*

If you really drew that "ahh" sound out, that exhale was the longest. You might have even wondered how long it was going to take. The longer you exhale, the more the receptors in the lungs are triggered. The more receptors that are triggered, the more they tell the nervous system to turn on the Calm Brain response. This is how we can hack the nervous system to calm ourselves down. Pretty nifty!

Going back to our Bhāvanā practice from the last chapter, we are utilizing mantra and the breath to create a desired outcome in the body. This is yet another way to hack into the nervous system! The Bhāvanā practice uses 4:4:6 count breath – inhaling for four counts, retaining the breath for four counts, and exhaling for six counts (or longer) using sound. This supports the nervous system in activating the Calm Brain effect, which helps us to calm, soothe, learn, retain information, and even relax. While this practice has not been studied (yet), try it for yourself, with and without sound. When you adjust for making sound, which can feel weird at first, you will find that the sound makes all the difference.

LifeForce Yoga Mantra

In this section, you will find a list of all the mantras we use in LifeForce Yoga. This is to help familiarize you with them. These mantras are then incorporated into the practices in the rest of this manual. All the mantras that we use in LifeForce Yoga are non-devotional. You are of course welcome to use a devotional mantra if that is what supports you most.

Chakra Mantras

There are two types of chakra mantras, those that energize and those that calm. The energizing chakra mantras are called *bīja* (pronounced bee-ja), meaning seed. These seed sounds awaken and increase the element that is associated with that chakra. We will talk more about the chakras when we cover meditation in Chapter Eight. A note about pronunciation of the mantras. In Sanskrit, the "a" sound is an "ah" sound, so the word mantra is pronounced "mahn-trah," the word Sanskrit is pronounced "sahn-skrit," and all of the bīja mantras that follow, while written as Lam, or Vam, sound more like Lum, or Vum. The chakra sounds can be long and drawn out, which is meditative. They can also be repeated in a quick fashion, which is more energizing. We will explore these options in later chapters, for now we will simply learn the sounds.

- Lam increases the element of Earth, is grounding, and is used for the first chakra
- Vam increases the element of Water, is flowing, and is used for the second chakra
- Ram increases the element of Fire, is heating, and is used for the third chakra
- Yam increases the element of Air, is light, and is used for the fourth chakra
- Ham increases the element of Space, is expansive, and is used for the fifth chakra
- Om is used for the sixth chakra
- Ng (like at the end of the word gong) is used for the seventh chakra

The calming mantras are a set of soothing vowel sounds. Because these mantras are meant to be cooling, calming, and soothing, we hold these vowel sounds for a long period.

- Ō, pronounced oh, is used for the first chakra
- Ū, pronounced ooo is used for the second chakra
- Ah is used for the third chakra
- Ā, pronounced eh, is used for the fourth chakra
- Ē, pronounced eee, is used for the fifth chakra
- M, pronounced mm, is used for the sixth chakra
- Hing is used for the seventh chakra.

Other Mantras

These other mantras are non-devotional and used for the Bhāvanā practice, in yoga postures, and during meditation practices. Some of these you will find used in practices discussed in this manual. Some you will find in videos on our YouTube channel or in the store.

- *Om* is the universal mantra that is said to be the sound of creation.

- *Hrīm*, pronounced "hreem," is an empowerment mantra that brings about joy, ecstasy, and bliss and energizes the heart.
- *So-ham* can be translated to "I am that."
- *Ma-ha-ha* is one of the vyāhriti mantras used to awaken the heart.
- *Shanti* is the Sanskrit word for peace. When used in mantra practice it is often repeated three times.

Other Sounds

In addition to the mantras listed above, we also use sound combinations. These are like mantras however they lack any specific meaning. They are combinations of sounds to evoke a specific feeling or bhāvanā in the user. The following are often used in movements during a LifeForce Yoga practice, as well as during the Bhāvanā practice.

- Ma-ha-ra, used to evoke calm strength
    - Combines the soothing sound of ma with the energizing sounds of ha and ra
- Ma-ha-ya, used to evoke an energized heart
    - Combines the soothing sound of ma, with the energizing sound of ha, and the sound for the heart, ya
- Sha-ma-ya, used to evoke a sense of peace
    - Combines the soothing sounds of sha and ma, with the sound of the heart, ya
- Dhi-ri-ha, pronounced dhee-ree-ha, used to evoke strength
    - All three sounds are energizing, especially when sounding with force

Revisit Chapter Three on Bhāvanā for the list of bhāvanās and which of the above sounds to use during your practice.

Mantra as a Portal into Meditation

Due to the power of mantra to focus and direct the mind, it is a beautiful portal into meditation. All mantra has this power. While there is no specific answer or research for why, mantras in Sanskrit form seem to be more effective at this than other languages. It may simply be that because we do not speak the language or fully understand the words, that it has a more powerful effect. My personal belief is that these mantras are vibrating at DNA level.

In the beginning, we start by chanting the mantra aloud as this helps to hold the attention and focus. We then begin to soften the mantra to a whisper and the silently, yet the mouth still moves to form the mantra. When we chant without making sound, this is called *upamshu*. This is said to be 1,000 times more powerful than chanting aloud. When the mind is tranquil during the practice of *upamshu*, then the transition is made to mental repetition of the mantra. The mental repetition is said to be 1,000 times more powerful than upamshu. Please know that you may need to chant the mantra aloud for years before being able to do the mental repetition without disruptions from the mind.

LifeForce Yoga Heart Mantra

In every LifeForce Yoga course, we use a special mantra to connect and honor our hearts as an expression of connection to our Inner Radiance and each other. We chant this mantra at the end of sessions as well as during meditation sessions. It can be challenging to learn a longer mantra from the pages of a book (you are welcome to chant the English translation instead). You can find a recording of this chant as well as instruction on pronunciation on my album *Mantra Chanting with Rose*, available on iTunes, Spotify, and other streaming services.

Experience: Ātma hṛdaye

This chant is a refrain that is part of a larger mantra found in the Taittiriya Brahmana. The chant invites the natural elements to support the organs creating good health. This is a chant to the heart from the heart. It is the heart's true nature to love for no reason at all, without conditions or judgment. Abiding in the heart's true nature we understand that there is no separation between love and bliss and wholeness. Chanting this mantra with this essence in mind we can come to know the deepest wisdom of the heart, the oneness of being.

Sanskrit (pronunciation)
Ātma hṛdaye (aht-ma hri-dah-yay)
Hṛdayam mayi (hri-dah-yum mah-ee)
Aham amṛte (ah-hum ahm-ri-tay-eh)
Amṛtam anāndam brahmāni (ahm-ri-tum ah-nan-dum brah-mah-nee)

Translation
My true nature is the heart. The heart is my true nature.
I am the bliss of the heart. The Heart that I am is the unending bliss of Oneness.

Self-Inquiry Question/Writing Prompt:
- What does the oneness of the heart mean to me?
- How do I express my heart's true nature?

Tips for Practicing Mantra
Traditionally the best times for practicing mantra and meditation are at sunrise, facing East, and sunset, facing West. It is said that the breath and mind come into a natural balance at sunrise and sunset. The traditional duration of practice is 108 repetitions. Use a mala, a strand of 108 beads to help you keep track of mantra repetitions. If you choose to take on a mantra

practice, commit to doing one mantra for several weeks, so that you can see the results of that mantra.

Summary

The brain processes hundreds of billions of bits of information each second in the form of sensory input and thoughts. The more aware of this processing we are, the more distracted and uncomfortable our experience. Mantra is a tool to support to focus the mind, helping to create an experience of ease and peace. LifeForce Yoga uses non-devotional Sanskrit mantras to connect to bhāvanā and instill different energies in the body.

CURRENT MOOD – UNBALANCED AS F
UNDERSTANDING YOUR MOOD

I had been doing yoga for years. When I practiced at home, I did the poses but never the resting at the end; I HATED *śavasana* (pronounced sha-va-sa-na) with a passion. In fact, I disliked all the parts of yoga where I had to be still for more than a minute. They were filled with discomfort, pain, and anxiety. The moment we would pause or sit for meditation, my mind was spinning and flooded with thoughts. As someone who was suffering from Obsessive Compulsive Disorder, those thoughts were out of control, my dog was off the leash, so to speak.

Worse still was *śavasana*; lie down and be still for minutes, sometimes as much as 10 minutes, with strangers around me. Lying there, mind racing and feeling like ants were crawling on my body was torture. I would do my best not to scratch my face or my arms because I knew that Amy was sitting there and watching. I did not want her to see me failing at the what I thought had to be the simplest part of yoga (I was wrong). I would fight the urge until it became overwhelming and then I would scratch. My favorite part was becoming the part where she would bring us out of the practice. Ah, such sweet relief.

I loved the class! Amy was sweet and welcoming. I did not feel judged by her. The other people in the class were nice, even if I did not know their names. I even had my usual spot. There was a lot of movement, it was challenging, and even the weird sounds were fun.

I was making yoga friends in a yoga study group I had joined. We decided to go take a class at a yoga studio that was unfamiliar to me. The other people in the group all practiced at Yoga Oasis and I thought I would give it a try. The class was intermediate, and I figured that I could do the poses and hang with it. The teacher worked us so hard during the class. I concentrated on the practice and felt laser focused. After what felt like forever, we got to the dreaded *śavasana*. For once, I was a little excited; I was exhausted after the intense practice. She played some music that was a bunch of guys chanting Om. I laid there and felt still. My mind was too tired to obsess, and I drifted off a little bit.

In LifeForce Yoga terms, my mood had finally been met. What I needed was to burn off all that excess mental and emotional energy that I was carrying around. Once that energy was gone, I could come to a place where ease and relaxation existed. That class was a game changer because it alerted me to the possibility that there was beyond my racing mind — relaxation. I would chase that experience for years until I learned to accept whatever the current experience was. Once I found that acceptance, I stopped running away from meditation and *savasana*. The key was and is meeting the mood.

What is the Mood?

Mood is a temporary state of mind or feeling. This could be on a physical, energetic, emotional, mental, or even spiritual level. The important part of understanding the mood, is that it is fleeting and changeable. In some cases, we understand that. When we are tired, we know that if we rest, we will be less tired (excepting certain health issues). When we are hangry, we know that food will set us right. But what about when we are feeling anxious, or depressed? We can get stuck in those moods, believing that anxiety or depression is all we are.

The yogis believe that depression and anxiety are the result of constricted *Prāna*, or life force. *Pra* means to "bring forth" and *na* means the "eternal cosmic vibration." Prāna is the universal life force energy of the divine that moves within us. Harkening back mantra, prāna is the vibrational energy wave that we connect with every time we make sacred sound. To understand the relationship between mood, energy, and our bodies from the yogic perspective, we need to explore the foundations of yogic philosophy.

Foundations of Yogic Philosophy

Sāmkhya Philosophy is the foundation of all yoga. Sāmkhya, meaning number, enumerates the categories of existence. There are two main categories. Purusha is the transcendental self and is sometimes called the "seer." It is unchanging consciousness, or witness consciousness, that existed before life took form. Prakriti is defined as matter, nature, or the material world, and is the "seen," by the seer. It is everything that is not purusha. It is said that purusha can see but cannot walk, and prakriti can walk but cannot see. Yoga is the reunification of purusha and prakriti.

Prāna is the direct and subtle link between purusha and prakriti. When prana is allowed to flow and connect purusha and prakriti we come to a state of wholeness. Most of the time, our prāna is constricted. The main constrictions come in the form of the gunas, which can be defined as the "qualities of nature." The gunas are the different forms that all energy takes, including our own. Before we delve into the complex topic of the gunas, let's explore how sāmkhya philosophy defines the body.

The Sheaths

First introduced in the *Taittiriya Upanishad* more than 3,000 years ago, the kośas (pronounced ko-shas), meaning "sheaths," are a foundation for understanding that we are more than body and mind. The ancient seers saw that there were sheathes, layers, or bodies that surrounded and even prevented us from knowing our true essence as the transcendental self, the spirit, or the Inner Radiance. They are often pictured as Russian nesting dolls. We experience freedom AND constriction in each of these sheaths. LifeForce Yoga is a means of releasing the constrictions and allowing freedoms.

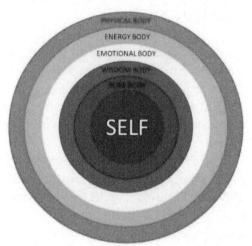

The first and densest sheath, or body, is the *annamaya kośa,* or the food sheath. This is the existence of the physical body. It is called the food body because it is made of up what we eat. Separation is experienced in this sheath as physical blocks and constrictions. This might show up as muscle soreness, physical pain, disease, holding the breath, illness, or anything emanating from the physical body that distracts us from full awareness of Inner Radiance.

The next layer is the *prānamaya kośa*, known as the energy body. While Prāna is the subtle and direct link between Purusha and Prakrti, prāna (with a small p) is the specific energy that pervades the body. You experience this energy in the breath and the subtle pulses of energy in the limbs, as well as head rushes, tingling, feeling grounded, etc. Separation is experienced in this body as a feeling of constricted energy or uncontrolled energy.

The next sheath is called the *manomaya kośa*, known as the thinking, judgmental, emotional, and reactive mind. This is the sheath of sense perception, reactions (as opposed to responding), judgements of self and others, feelings, emotions, patterns of behavior, and thoughts. We experience constriction in this sheath as obsessive thoughts patterns, negative self-talk, overthinking, and comparison.

The next layer is the *vijñānamaya kośa*, known as the wisdom or discerning body. This is the level of faith and spiritual understanding, where wisdom is known within every cell in the body. Here the mind communicates in thoughts, beliefs, and images. Constrictions at this level are experienced as core beliefs and systems to which we cling. These are usually beliefs around self-worth, deserving, and self-love.

The fifth and final envelope is the *ānandamaya kośa*, known as the bliss body, is the last layer of constriction that surrounds the Inner Radiance. It is not such a bad place to get stuck, for it is the sheath of "superlative happiness," "joy," and "peaceful equanimity." This is where we experience oneness with the creative source and divine intelligence. Yet, it is still a layer of separation around our transcendental self. Constriction at this level can be experienced as hyper-spirituality all the way to a complete lack of connection.

These layers surround our experience of Purusha and can keep us from experiencing our innate wholeness. Even though we can have many layers of constrictions, we can also connect with our Inner Radiance through practices that help us dive beneath those layers. A constriction does not mean that you are disconnected, nor that there is something wrong with you. Think of a constriction as a distraction that pulls your attention away from the truth of reality, which is oneness with Divine essence.

Self-Inquiry Questions/Writing Prompts for the Kośas

1. How is my body feeling today? Are there areas that feel uncomfortable or painful? How is my breath showing up? (annamaya kosha)
2. How is my energy level? (prānamaya kosha)
3. What thoughts & emotions are present? (manomaya kosha)
4. What core belief, perhaps taken on in childhood, is influencing my actions today? (vijnānamaya kosha)
5. What can I do to clear constrictions in my body-mind to experience more joy, bliss & love? (ānandamaya kosha)

What are the Constrictions that Show Up in the Five Bodies?

These constrictions are known as *kleshas*, which means "affliction." These are the painful waves that rise and fall in the mind and radiate into the other bodies. Through the process of yoga these afflictions are brought to the surface and cleansed from the system. There are five kleshas.

1. Avidyā, meaning to "not see the oneness of our true nature," is simply translated as "ignorance." This is the mistaken belief of separation, the illusion that we are not connected to each other or our Inner Radiance. It is that feeling of loneliness.

2. Asmitā, means "egoism." Because we feel alone and separate, we begin to cling to apparent reality. This is identifying ourselves by what we do and who we are to others, as opposed to who we really are. Some cling to roles and identities, others to material objects. This mind wave causes us pain in the sense that we get stuck in a role. For example, "who am I, if I am not a mother, or cancer survivor, or a member of a political party, or a disease?"

3. Rāga, means "desire" or "attachment." Rāga arises because we experience pleasure or positive reinforcement around a behavior or an experience. When this happens, we NEED to repeat it, or we start to feel bad or disconnected. This is not the good parts of being attached, the way that a child is attached to a parent. Rāga is the behavior that keeps us stuck in unhealthy behaviors or thought patterns. As

one yogi said, "there is nothing wrong with attachment, only the need to repeat it."

4. Dvesha, meaning "to divide life," simply translated as "aversion," is the klesha of pushing things away. This is the flip side of rāga. When we have an unpleasant experience, we can throw up a wall so that we do not repeat this experience. These aversions can be big or small. We could have a bad experience at a restaurant and so we never go back to that restaurant. Maybe someone was rude to us and now we refuse to have anything to do with that person. Think about all the "bad" experiences that you have had in life and the lengths to which you go to not repeat those experiences, sometimes to the extent that your quality of life suffers.

5. Abhinivesha is the final klesha and means "clinging to life/change" and "fear of death." Our patterns of behavior arise around maintaining our life exactly as it is. Change is stressful and upsetting to the system, even when it is desired change. A new job, a new home, a marriage, these are often things that we seek out, yet when we are in the midst of the change, we become uncomfortable. The ultimate fear of change is death because it is a permanent change and moving into the unknown. This fear goes beyond our natural inclinations to keep ourselves safe. Not walking into traffic is not a painful mind wave, it is smart. It becomes a painful mind wave when we refuse to cross a street, even when no cars are present.

The kleshas come together to form the constrictive bubble of personality/ego to which we cling. This is the unhealthy ego that exerts its desires on others, not the healthy ego that draws boundaries and makes sure that you are healthy and safe.

A Basic Understanding of Emotional Energy from the Yogic Perspective

In LifeForce Yoga, we talk about the human experience from the standpoint of energy. Our energy takes different forms, the gunas, in the five layers of our being: physical, subtle, emotional, mental, and spiritual. According to Yogic philosophy, the gunas, meaning "attributes," are the building blocks of nature, the different ways all energy shows up. There are three gunas: *tamas*, *rajas*, and *sattva*. They form our physical, energetic and emotional worlds. To bring ourselves back our innate experience wholeness, we must balance the energy that is present. We call this practice Meeting the Mood. When we meet the mood, we are more receptive to the practices that work. In other words, "a spoonful of sugar helps the medicine go down."

The Heaviness of Tamas

Tamas, means "darkness," is the quality of inertia and the constriction of heaviness and lethargy. Tamas can show up as physical lethargy, energetic tiredness, tamped down emotions, mental sluggishness, and disconnection. It becomes constrictive when it manifests as disinterest, disinclination toward constructive activity, sadness, depression, lack of feeling, and a sense of separation. When a person gets stuck in tamas, it becomes labeled as a disorder. The energy of tamas needs lightness and flow.

Tamasic disorders: depression, major depressive disorder, seasonal affective disorder, catatonia, etc.

Assessing tamas: sluggish body movements, drooping eyelids, collapsed shoulders, slouching, very relaxed posture, yawning, no visible breath movements, sighing, talking slowly, mumbling, etc.

Some key words that identify the tamasic mood:

- Depressed
- Lethargic
- Frozen
- Hopeless
- Daydreaming
- Collapse
- Exhausted
- Sluggish
- Numb

Working with tamas: meet the inertia by starting slower with gentle movements increasing activity and energy.

Experience: Early Morning Experiment for Building Energy (5 minutes):

The next time you wake up and feel tired, open your eyes and take six deep breaths in and out. Bend your knees and bring your feet flat to the bed. Inhale and exhale bring your knees to the right. Inhale to center, exhale to the left. Go back and forth like this, with strong breaths in and out three more times on each side. When you finish, come back to center and take three more breaths and notice if you feel a little more awake and if the hips and low back feel a little more awake. Press yourself up so that you are sitting on the edge of your bed. Inhale and reach your arms up over your head, spreading the fingers wide. Exhale with the sound "ram" (pronounced "rum") as you bring your arms out to your side and down to the bed, allowing the hands to lightly hit the bed. Inhale reach up, exhale with "ram" to bring the arms down to the bed four more times. When you finish, take three breaths noticing the hands and fingers, the breath, and if you feel more awake. You can use this practice anywhere, when you need to a little more energy.

The Intensity of Rajas

Rajas, meaning "excited," is the quality of energy and the constriction of frenetic and/or excessive movement. Rajas manifests as movement, energy, and awakeness. It becomes constrictive when it manifests as restlessness, distraction, reactivity, nervousness, anxiety, agitation, chattiness, racing mind, emotional overflow, feeling too much, and lack of boundaries. When a person gets stuck in rajas, it is labeled as a disorder.

Rajasic disorders: generalized anxiety disorder, ADHD (attention deficit hyperactivity disorder), panic disorder, agoraphobia, social anxiety, mania, obsessive compulsive disorder, and PTSD (post-traumatic stress disorder).

Assessing rajas: quick movements, fidgeting, playing/moving objects, rapid breathing, gasping for air when talking, rapid speech, wide eyes, darting eyes, inability to focus, distracted, rigid body posture, thrusting chest forward, etc.

Trauma and PTSD fall under the category of rajas, because of the energetic experience of being "exposed" or "a raw nerve." When we suffer from trauma/PTSD we may shut ourselves off and show up as tamasic and even carry a diagnosis of depression. We always want to keep in mind the "raw nerve" aspect of trauma. This means that practices meant to stimulate tamas and wake us up can also overstimulate and overwhelm us when we have trauma/PTSD. If you know you have a history of trauma, go slow with the practices that stimulate/energize and focus on the practices that help you ground. You will find more tools in the coming chapters.

Some key words that help you identify the rajasic mood:

- Anger
- Agitation
- Panic
- Anxious
- Uptight
- Frenetic
- Fighting
- Exhaustion
- Overwhelmed
- Confused

Working with rajas: meet the activity with vigorous movement and decrease the activity by grounding and slowing down.

Experience: Burning off the Excess Energy Experiment (5 minutes):

In a standing or seated position, inhale the arms up overhead and bring shoulders to your ears. Using the sound of "ah," exhale and lower the arms to your sides or lap with a gentle slap. Inhale and bring the arms up, exhale with 'ah' to bring the arms down. As you do this three more times, draw the sound of 'ah' out and the movement for as long as you can relaxing your shoulders as you lower. When you finish, if it is comfortable, close your eyes and take three deep breaths, noticing if your shoulders feel a little softer, if your hands feel a light or tingly. Either seated or lying down, begin gentle twists from side to side, inhaling to center, exhaling as you rotate. Go slow and invite your eyes to soften or close. When you have completed six on each side, come back to center, rest the eyes, and take six long slow breaths, lengthening the exhale. When you finish, notice how your feet feel on the floor, the sensation of your body against the floor (or chair), and if you feel a little calmer. You can do this anytime you need to calm or even as a practice for bed.

You may have noticed that both of those experiments used the same movements and breath, but in a different order. That is because it is not the practices but the order of the practices. You can use the same five, or ten, practices when working with lethargy or excessive energy. The way you order the practices is what makes the difference. Pretty cool, huh?

The Evenness of Balance

Sattva is the third guna and means "beingness." It is the principle of "lucidity or sheer existence devoid of conceptual filters and emotional overlays." (Georg Feuerstein, Encyclopedic Dictionary of Yoga). This is the quality of balance, or peace of mind that remains undisturbed by stimulus. Resting in sattva is one of the goals of yoga. When we do our practices, sattva is the first step on the path to liberation.

Because sattva is a guna, it is still a constriction. If you are going to have constrictions, balance is a pretty nice place to live. For those on the spiritual path to enlightenment (which is the ultimate destination of the yogi), the gunas must be transcended to achieve Self-realization. For those that are seeking a respite from the ups and downs, let sattva be the place you rest.

Understanding the Movement of the Gunas

We are dynamic beings and as such, we experience all three of the gunas during the day. Even someone that is stuck in a guna will still experience the others at some point during the day. Think back over your day. Did you experience a moment of tiredness or lethargy? Did you experience a moment of energy or stress? The individual who experiences major depressive disorder still has moments of energy, of being awake. It may be a fleeting moment that goes unnoticed, but it is there. Unless you are a rock, you will experience energy in some form.

Here is an example of the movement of the gunas:

Mike wakes up in the morning and he is tired (tamas). He drinks a cup of coffee and feels awake (rajas). Midmorning he starts to get tired again (tamas), so he has another cup of coffee to wake himself up (rajas). Midafternoon he experiences lethargy (tamas) and he gets a candy bar, rather than coffee (rajas). He gets home from work and feels wound up and thinking about work (rajas) and drinks some wine to help him relax (tamas). As Mike gets ready for bed he is thinking about work and knows that he will not be able to get to sleep (rajas), so he takes a sleeping aid (tamas). When he wakes up in the morning, he is exhausted (tamas) and drinks a coffee (rajas) and the cycle starts again.

Mike went back and forth between tamas and rajas all day. He may have had moments of sattva, but if he did it was not a result of the coffee or the alcohol. To achieve sattva, Mike needed a balancing practice, like a breath, or sound, or posture. He needed something first thing in the morning to meet his mood and then energize. Mike needed something at night to get rid of some energy and then to soothe. The more that we can give our bodies what they need and then help them balance, the more we can release our dependencies on the outside world. When you use the LifeForce Yoga practices, you are using tools that you carry all the time.

Self-Inquiry: What is My Guna?

	Tamas	Rajas	Sattva
Speech	Slow/Slurred	Rapid/Breathless	Even
Posture	Defeated, caved	Propped, forward	Upright
Complexion	Sallow	Flushed	Radiant
Eyes	1,000 Mile Stare	Darting	Relaxed
	Vacant/Avoidant	Intense Stare	Eye Contact
Mouth/lips	Slack	Pursed	Easy Smile
	Dry	Chewing lips	Relaxed
Jaw	Slack or gaping	Clenched	Relaxed
Nostrils	No breath movement	Flared	Normal
Forehead	Furrowed with worry	Furrowed with anger	Relaxed
Shoulders	Slumped	Tense	Relaxed
Hands	Limp	Wringing/Clenched	Relaxed
Chest	Sunken	Thrust forward	Normal
Legs	Heavy or sprawled	Tense/crossed/bouncing	Normal
Feet	Limp	Moving	Normal
Breath	Shallow	Intense	Deep Breaths
	Uneven	Uneven	Even
	Non-existent or sighs	Rapid or gasping	Even
	Upper chest	Rib cage	Full or abdominal
Movements	Sluggish	Jerky	Calm
	Slow	Rapid	Even
	Unengaged	Forced	Steady
Emotions	Repressed	Overexpressed	Expressed
	Suppressed	Fully blown	Expressed
	Fear	Aggression	Calm
	Confusion	Contradictoriness	Clear
	Despondency	Blame	Accepting
	Grief	Opinionated	Understanding
	Sadness	Exhaustion	Calm
	Depression	Anxiety	Peaceful
	Hopeless	Greed	Focused
Mind	Lethargic	Overactive	Clear
	Unaware	Hypervigilant	Present
	Slow	Jumping	Even
	Clouded	Unfocused	Focused
	Depressed	Anxious	Clear

Use the tool above to support you in determining what guna is present. Trust your intuition to know which guna is the most dominant in any moment.

Summary

In LifeForce Yoga, we view the mood as a fluctuation of energy. We drop the label of the diagnosis to understand that we can experience our energies in many forms. Our energy may be constricted and/or heavy (tamas). Or it could be expressed and/or frantic (rajas). Most, if not all of us, would prefer it to be balanced (sattva). These forms of energy are experienced as constrictions in the physical, subtle, emotional, mental, or spiritual bodies and keep us from being fully connected with our Inner Radiance.

LifeForce Yoga teaches that we meet our moods right where they are. We might be resting or burning off excess energy. When we meet the mood, we are more likely to follow through with the interventions, or practices, that lead us to our desired outcome of energy. To remain connected to our Inner Radiance, we must commit to this method of working with ourselves.

LIFTING THE WEIGHT
TOOLS FOR ELEVATION

I am feeling hopeless and alone. I know I am not alone; my friends reach out and my husband is in the other room. The crushing weight of life has left me flattened. It is nothing in particular, I just cannot handle anything. All I want to do is crawl into bed and take a nap. I work hard, so I can even justify crawling into bed in the middle of the day.

Instead, I keep pushing and find myself crawling down the rabbit hole of this dark energy. I wonder if I have ever really been happy. Maybe when I felt "happy" it was just a momentary flash because really, underneath everything I am sad and alone. I try to recall times when I felt happy and connected. Even as those memories arise, I see the darkness that lives underneath them, like a creature under the bed waiting to grab my ankles and devour me. Instead of lying down, I convince myself that I only need a break and I turn to YouTube.

I have this rule, a very important rule in my office. If I turn on YouTube for more than a video, it means that I need to walk away from my desk and do something else. Today is one of the days that I remember this rule and I put my computer to sleep. The part of me that has been practicing yoga for years says that I need to go to my yoga mat and let my practice unfold from there.

I lie down on my mat in my practice space. I sink into the mat and my eyes get soft. This is not about checking out, I know that I am here to breathe and reconnect with myself. I have forgotten who I really am, and my practice is that time to remember, to awaken the inner radiance that is my Divine self. As I lie on the mat, I take some deep breaths and ask my body what it needs most, and it responds "elevation."

Ah, elevation. I grab my Elevation essential oil, apply it to my chest, and put my bean bag bolster under my hips to come into legs up the wall (*viparita karani*), my favorite pose. Now that I am here, I start some intentional and deeper breathing. Already I am feeling more connected and at ease. The weight is starting to ease. I add my sankalpa of love and add my bhāvanā of feeling my heart as open as the universe to strengthen my connection to myself.

After ten minutes of breathing here, my eyes open and my body starts to move. Gentle and organic movements and adjustments that having me rolling around on the floor. I throw in some abdominal work because it always lights my fire. Then I come to a seated position and begin for quiet reflection and meditation with a hand gesture. All told, it has only been twenty minutes since I collapsed onto the mat under the weight of the world. I am lighter and brighter, feeling more at ease. It is not always this fast. After years of practice, I have built up the threshold for my practice. What once took my many intense breathing practices now take less time and effort. Every time I remind myself of my wholeness, my heart lifts and I remember my Inner Radiance. Just sharing and reading this short story has changed my mood. It does not take much but coming back to the practices works. And when it does not work, it is just time to go back to the proverbial drawing board.

You are an ocean. You can be gentle, stormy, and even get stuck in the doldrums. You could spend hours, days, months, and years in this state of lethargy, lacking motivation to do the simplest things. You might even be in this place right now. The most important thing to remember is that you are energy and by its nature, energy changes.

The yoga practice that lifts the weight of tamas is one that churns the waters of your ocean. The sludge that is holding you back is brought to the surface, where you can begin to release it. Keep churning that ocean and your gifts begin to arise.

Start with Where You Are

As we discussed in the last chapter, meeting yourself where you are is perhaps the most important aspect of the practice of LifeForce Yoga. In the case of tamas, this means practicing in your bed, or lying down on the floor for yoga. Yes, sun salutations would be great for building your energy, but how likely are you to get up and roll out a yoga mat when you feel this way? Going to a yoga class would be great, but if you do not have the energy to practice at home, how will you have the energy to get yourself to a yoga class? When you meet the heavy energy with a slow and gentle practice, your energy will begin to build, and you will be able to continue to more practice.

Self-Inquiry/Writing Prompt: Building a Bhāvanā for Energy

Your bhāvanā is your vision for energy in your life. Use the following questions as a guide to help you connect with the energy that lifts your mood.

- How would you like to experience your energy?

- What words would you use to describe this energy?

- When you have this kind of energy, where do you feel it in your body?

- Is there a specific image that encapsulates this energy? Maybe a symbol? An image from nature? Maybe something from your life?

- Perhaps drawing a picture or printing one out from the internet that represents how you would like your energy to show up.

- If you enjoy creating vision boards, spend some time building a vision board for the experience of energy you would like to cultivate in your life.

Stair Step Breath

Stair Step Breath is one of the most utilized breaths in LifeForce Yoga. It is a way to connect with the breath when we feel disconnected from it, or even afraid of the breath. This practice allows us to slowly and gently release constrictions around the breath and is a gateway to the other breathing practices of yoga.

There is always a good reason for why we are not breathing deeply. Yoga trainings encourage working with individuals to deepen the breath when it seems stuck. This is not bad, and it is a good idea to deepen the breath. But, if your first experience with yoga breathing causes you to feel anxious or brings all the sludge to the surface, it can be scary and make the breath harder to access. As you will experience, this breath builds length, depth, and energy.

Stair Step is an excellent early morning practice. On those days when I am too tired to get up, I roll on my back and practice stair step. This usually energizes me enough to start doing some yoga under the covers. The next thing I know, I am awake, and it is much easier to get out of bed.

Experience: Stair Step Breath for Energy (5 minutes)

Practice lying down or in a seated position. You can find audio for this practice at yogafordepression.com/stair-step-breath

1. *Allow the eyes to soften and breathe naturally.*
2. *Begin to connect with your bhāvanā for energy that you identified in the prior exercise.*
   a. *Exhale all the breath.*
3. *Begin by taking little steps up, through the nostrils*
   a. *When you get to the top, pause and invite your bhāvanā for energy.*
   b. *Slide down.*
   c. *Practice 1 – 2 more times.*
4. *This time take a smooth ride up.*
   a. *Pause and embrace your bhāvanā for energy.*
   b. *Little steps down, through the nostrils.*
   c. *Practice 3 – 5 more times.*
5. *This time, little steps up.*
   a. *Pause at the top and allow yourself to be filled with your bhāvanā for energy.*
   b. *Little steps down.*
   c. *Practice 3 – 5 more times.*
6. *This time, little steps up.*
   a. *Pause at the top and experience yourself as energy, awake, bright, and present.*
   b. *Slide down.*
7. *Allow the breath to return to normal.*
8. *Begin to balance the breath by imagining the breath moving in the body, from the crown of the head to the soles of the feet.*
   a. *Inhaling to the crown. Exhaling to the feet.*
   b. *If you wish, you can add affirmation.*
   c. *Inhale "I am" to the crown.*
   d. *Exhale "energized," or any other key word that keeps you in connection with your bhāvanā for energy.*
   e. *Do that two more times.*
9. *When you are ready, allow the eyes to find the horizon.*

Self-Inquiry Questions/Writing Prompt:

- Do you feel more connected with energy?
- Are you more awake?
- Was it easier to connect with your breath?
- Do you see yourself using the practice when you feel low on energy?

Energizing Mantra to Add to Movements and Meditations

Mantra is an excellent way to begin building the energy in your body. You encountered the different sound options in Chapter Four. Here we begin to weave them into the practices to help build energy. The sound options that work best when awakening and moving energy are the bīja mantras, lam, vam, ram, yam, ham, om, ng.

- Lam increases the element of Earth, is grounding, and is used for the first chakra
- Vam increases the element of Water, is flowing, and is used for the second chakra
- Ram increases the element of Fire, is heating, and is used for the third chakra
- Yam increases the element of Air, is light, and is used for the fourth chakra
- Ham increases the element of Space, is expansive, and is used for the fifth chakra
- Om is used for the sixth chakra
- Ng (like at the end of the word gong) is used for the seventh chakra

Vam, Ram, and Yam are especially beneficial for when you feel stuck, tamped down and disconnected. You can meet the mood with your body position in bed and add the sound which begin to awaken and move the energy. To put it another way, you meet the mood with your body position and in this case, the intervention to lift the mood are the sounds.

Other sounds to weave into your practice that help to elevate the mood are:

- Ma-ha-ra to connect with calm strength and calm energy
- Ma-ha-ya to connect with a strong heart
- Ma-ha-ha to connect to laughter and lightheartedness
- Dhi-ri-ha to connect with strength and courage

Experience: In Bed Practice (5 – 15 minutes)

Begin this practice with Stair Step Breath to help motivate you for movement. Practice with your eyes open as this will help to wake you up. If you practice with the eyes closed, you could fall back asleep (which is not necessarily a bad thing) or you could move into rumination (which could be more constricting).

Pavanamuktāsana *(pah-vah-nah-mook-tah-sa-nah) meaning "wind relieving pose" for the way it releases excess air element from the body, helping to ground:*

Bring your right knee into your chest, interlacing your fingers around the knee, or behind the knee if that is more comfortable. Feel free to bend the left knee, this will make things easier for the low back. Inhale and on the exhale, use the sound "lam" as you bring your right knee into your chest. Inhale soften, exhale with "lam" to bring the knee in. Two more times. You can make this a little more challenging by pressing the knee into the hands as though you are resisting the pressure of the hands. As you practice, you will feel muscles engaging in the hip joint.

This pose is good for getting the hip joint moving. The gentle pressure on the abdomen aids in facilitating elimination. Practice on both sides.

Supta pādāṅguṣṭāsana *(soup-tah pah-dahng-oos-tah-sah-nah) means"reclining big toe pose" because in its finished form the hand holds the toe as the leg is extended:*

Bring your right knee back into your chest and interlace your fingers behind the right knee. Inhale with the knee bent. Exhale and use the sound "lam" as you extend the sole of the right foot up towards the ceiling allowing the knee to straighten as feels comfortable. The left leg can be bent with the foot on the bed. Inhale and bend the knee, exhale and extend with "lam." Practice three to five more times.

If you wish, you can add a hip opener here, by extending the leg and then opening the whole leg out to the side. With every exhale, use the sound of "vam," to support the release and opening happening in the inner right hip and thigh muscles. To support your hip joints and low back, bend your left knee into your chest, hold

it with your left hand, and open it to the left. Hold this position for three breaths.

This pose helps to open the hamstrings and calf muscles, while gently strengthening the quadricep (front of the thigh) muscles. Practice on both sides.

Jathara parivartanāsana *(jah-tara par-ee-var-than-ah-sah-na) meaning "revolved abdominal pose" for this pose being an abdominal twist.*

There are two ways to practice this posture. The first is with both knees bent, the second in with one leg extended.

Bend both knees allowing the feet to rest on the bed. Inhale with the knees bent. Using the sound "ram," exhale and bring both knees to the right. Inhale to center. Exhale with "ram" and bring both knees to the left. Move back and forth. If you wish a little more activity, bring the knees into the chest first and then go from side to side. This requires a little more abdominal strength than keeping the feet on the bed.

Lengthen your right leg along the bed. Bend your left knee and bring the foot to rest on the right thigh, or on the bed next to your inner thigh. Bring your right hand to your outer left thigh. Inhale and with an exhale, begin to twist to the right with the sound of "ram." Hold the position for three to five breaths. Use an exhale to come back to center and switch sides.

Please be mindful with how intensely you stretch. More is not better. More can be damaging to your joints in the long term. One guide to keep you safe is if you feel the joints, you are likely stretching to much or too hard. We want our yoga practice to support us in the long term.

Get Moving

After that practice, you may be ready to get up and get moving. If you are not, repeat the movements until you feel ready to come into a seated position. You do not need to feel like you can take on the world. You just need to feel energized enough to come into a seated position to practice and energizing breath, or two. Then you can reevaluate whether you are ready to come into bigger movements with more energy.

Another key to movements that help break up the sludge of tamas that is keeping you in a lethargic state is to make movements dynamic. This means keep moving, however gently you would like. For example, in the In Bed practice above, the leg is constantly moving, instead of holding still. On the inhale, the leg is bent, on the exhale the leg extends. The addition of sound to the movement helps to keep things moving and waking up.

Energizing Yoga in Your Hands: Mudrās

The hands have the densest area of nerve receptors in the body at 2,500 nerve receptors per square centimeters. This density gives the hands a greater sensory experience than other parts of the body, with some exceptions. The hands take up a quarter of the area of the motor cortex of the brain. In the yogic tradition, the hands contain pathways for energy that align to the chakras and other parts of the energetic body (prānamaya kośa). Our energy is literally in our hands!

Mudrā, hand gestures and yoga practice for your hands, means "seal" or "gesture."

They are some of the best practices because they are portable and some of them can even be done in your pockets. If you do not have the energy to get up, you could try practicing a mudra that helps you build some energy.

Most of us are familiar with mudrās because we have seen them on statues. For instance, you may have seen the Buddha with his thumb and index finger touching and palms down on the knees. This is known as the *Chin Mudrā*, it is cooling, calming, and helps to focus the awareness for meditation. We are also familiar with the other mudrās. For example, the peace sign which was used in the 1960s to denote peace in the antiwar movement, is also called *Prāna Mudrā*. In LifeForce Yoga, we often refer to this mudrā as Happy Buddha Mudrā, and because it has both uplifting and calming effects. There is also the mudrā of aggression, which is most often seen in traffic — that extension of the middle finger in the air.

Therapeutic Application of Mudrās

Mudrās can be employed with the intent of loosening the grip of an emotion, constriction and/or limiting beliefs. Mudrās can also enhance a desired emotional, or energetic state. Indu Arora, author of *Mudrā: The Sacred Secret*, writes that for therapeutic application of mudrā it should be held for 45 minutes a day. The best way to complete 45 minutes in a day is to practice for 15 minutes three times a day. It takes 30 seconds for a mudrā to form the electrical magnetic frequency. Thus, we practice mudrās for 2 to 5 minutes, working up to longer practice.

In general, when the palms are facing up, the mudrās energizing. When the palms are facing down, the mudrā is grounding. There are several ways to use mudrās to support mood management. The first way, and more well-known way to use mudrās is during a meditation practice. Below are two mudrās that can be done to help you build your energy.

Brahma Mudrā – Gesture of Creation

Brahma mudrā helps us to tap into the creative force within us. This mudrā directs the breath, energy, and awareness into the solar plexus region which is the seed of our personal power and self-esteem. The solar plexus is the space between the navel and the lower ribs, is also, in yoga, the home of our digestive fire. It is this digestive fire that it energizes our entire system, while supporting the transformation of our experiences into wisdom. Brahma Mudrā awakens a deeper sense of personal power, self-esteem, determination, and that inner fire that sustains and drives us. When we are feeling tamasic (depressed, sad, low energy, lethargic, tired, etc.), Brahma Mudrā helps to start moving the energy. It also helps to increase determination; when you are lacking energy, a little bit of determination goes a long way. *Caution: if you suffer from hypertension, un-medicated high blood pressure, practice this with caution, or you can practice a mudrā with similar effects, like Matangi.*

Experience: The Gesture of Creativity

Come into a seated position where the spine can be long. Bring the hands in front of the torso with the palms facing up. Place the thumbs into the centers of the palms and curl the fingers around the thumbs. Press the knuckles and the first digits of all the fingers into each other so that the thumb portion of the fist is away from the body and the inner wrists face upwards. Feel free to add a little isometric pressure between the hands so the arms begin to feel strong. Make sure that there is space between the hand gesture at the navel and abdomen.

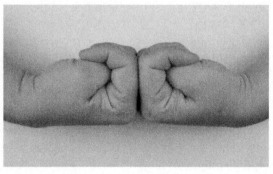

Soften the eyes and begin to deepen the breath. Allow the breath to follow the path of least resistance. As you breathe, begin to cultivate a connection with energy growing in the abdomen. You may wish to visualize a ball of energy, experience a warmth in the abdomen, or a repetition of the word energy. With every breath, imagine this energy growing brighter, feeding the rest of your being. This energy is like the sun nourishing your personal energy and vitality. Imagine this a radiant energy warming you from the inside out. Strengthen this inner radiance by using the sound for the third chakra, the tone of "ram." Take a deep breath in… "ram." Feel the tone of ram vibrate through the whole abdomen. Now increase in the energy, by repeating the sound of "ram" five times on two out breaths. Inhale…"ram, ram, ram, ram, ram." Do this one more time, feel the repetition of sound as stoking that inner radiant sun. Inhale…"ram, ram, ram, ram, ram." Experience this radiant inner energy as brighter, more awake. Envision your personal energy and vitality as a little brighter, more awake.

Use this radiant energy that is awakening vitality, energy, self-esteem, and determination to nourish the seeds of your heartfelt prayer, your sankalpa. That seed that your heart is planting your personal and spiritual growth. Imagine this radiant energy shining down on the garden of the heart, warming that seed planted within the heart. With every breath, imagine that this seed is cracking open and growing. Experience this seed that you have planted on the altar of your heart, as blooming in your life.

Allow the hands to fall open on the lap as you release the mudrā and allow the breath to return to normal. Sense the palms of the hands; the left palm and fingers, the right palm and fingers. Sense the arms. The face, the lips, left cheek, and right cheek. Perhaps you are aware of your energy as a little brighter. Perhaps aware of your vitality.

Self-Inquiry Questions/Writing Prompts:

- How did you experience your connection to energy? Was it an image, a feeling, or a word?
- What does your energy feel like after this practice?
- Did you experience a change in your mood?

Mātangi Mudrā – Gesture of Transformation

In Hindu mythology, Mātangi is the goddess of transformation and a manifestation of divine mother energy. She said to live in the throat and represents inner knowledge. This hand gesture supports us in cultivating wisdom and creativity from our life experiences. In other words, this is the mudrā of turning lemons into lemonade. This hand gesture helps you to awaken and then harness the energy in your solar plexus. When we are tamasic, our energy is tamped down. Using this mudrā invites that energy to begin to awaken. If you begin to feel light-headed or dizzy, this is your body telling you that your energy is moving.

Experience: The Gesture of Transformation

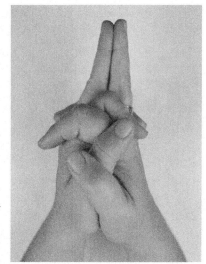

Come into a position where the spine can be long. Interlace the hands with the fingers on the outside and the right thumb on top. Extend to the middle fingers allowing the whole finger to touch while keeping the palms of the hands touching. Rest the shoulders down, elbows at the sides. You may rest the wrists against the solar plexus region, between the navel and base of the ribcage. For more energy, bring the hands of couple of inches in front of the body and rest forearms against the abdomen.

Soften the eyes and move into breath awareness. Feel the expansion of the inhale and the contraction of the exhale. Notice that the breath is drawn into the abdominal and solar plexus region. On the inhale, feel the breath spread out horizontally from the solar plexus region. On the exhale, feel the breath come together in the center of the body. Noticing the breath in the solar plexus, you also feel movement in the kidneys, the adrenals, and the back of the body. Maybe even a sense of warmth through the center of the body.

Begin to imagine heat, like a fire burning in the hearth of the abdomen. With every breath, this fire begins to strengthen and grow. It is the fire of transformation. As you imagine this fire of transformation growing, perhaps there is a color. Perhaps there is a shape, or an image. Imagine now that the warmth of this fire travels upwards into the throat region. As this energy rises, feel it and allow it to bring about a sense of clarity. To support this transformation, we use the sounds for the solar plexus region, the heart, and the throat. The sounds are "ram," "yam," and "ham," with an emphasis on the consonant at the beginning of the sound. Roll these three sounds together on three exhales. Inhale…"ram, yam, ham." Two more times. Inhale… "ram, yam, ham." Feel the vibrations arising from the navel up towards the throat and make the sounds one more time. Inhale… "ram, yam, ham". Allow yourself a moment to bask in the rising radiant energy of transformation, to experience the expansion of clarity.

Continue to hold Mātangi Mudrā, as you envision your heartfelt prayer, that seed that the heart has planted for your personal and spiritual growth. Perhaps envision with clarity how this seed blooms and grows in your life. Allow the energy from the mudrā to nourish and support your heartfelt prayer for three more breaths.

Release the mudrā. Rest the hands in the lap with palms open towards the ceiling; allow the breath to return to normal. Sense the palms of the hands. The left palm and fingers, the right palm and fingers. Maybe you experience vibrant energy, tingling, and radiance in the palms and fingers. It may feel as though you are still holding the Mudrā. Perhaps the experience of vibrant energy in the body is a sense of awakening and clarity. When you feel complete allow the eyes to open.

Self-Inquiry Questions/Writing Prompts:

- How did you experience your connection to this fire of transformation? Was it an image, a feeling, or a word?
- What does your energy feel like after this practice?
- Did you experience a change in your mood?

Energizing Prāṇāyāma

Once the body has moved you may be ready to move from a lying down position to a seated position for some breathing practices that help to wake you up and move your energy. The breath is a link between the body and the mind. The breath reflects the state of the mind and through the breath, we can control the mind. The western medical model tells us that breathing is the only involuntary function that we can also control. You are breathing without thinking about it and when you want, you can change the course of the breath.

Prāṇāyāma is the yogic word for changing the breath and is the regulation of breath and energy. Prāṇa is that direct link between the body, mind, and spirit. When we begin to regulate this energy, we can connect with our true essence with ease. Our true essence is free from constriction and the more we are in connection with our true essence the less we suffer.

The breathing exercises listed in this chapter are meant to energize and awaken. Go slow as you begin to explore these practices. Some people are extra sensitive to energizing practices and a little can go a long way. Please note that there are cautions listed at the end of each practice. As always, contact your doctor to make sure that these practices are appropriate for you. It is always helpful to work with a LifeForce Yoga Practitioner as they are trained in the application of these techniques. A list of practitioners can be found on yogafordepression.com.

Experience: Bellows Breath (1 – 2 minutes)

Bhastrikā is translated as bellows because the breath moves like a bellows that you might use on a fire. The breath itself does indeed stoke the fire of energy within you. This is a modified version of the traditional practice, which is even more intense. You can practice this seated on the edge of your bed after you have done a little movement. You can also practice this breath in any seated position, either on the floor or in a chair.

- *Sit with spine erect.*
- *Make fists with your hands and bring them to the inside of your shoulders with the forearms hugging the chest, and thumb and knuckles facing out.*

- *Take a normal natural breath in and out.*
- *As you inhale through the nostrils, send your arms straight up, over your head with great force as you open your palms out to the front, spreading your fingers wide.*

- o *If your shoulders are uncomfortable, you can send your arms straight out in front.*

> o *If you have a shoulder injury, you might just open and close the arms in front of the shoulders.*

- *Exhale with through the nostrils as you bring your hands & arms back to the starting position, making fists with your hands.*
- *Do this at a pace of one breath per second, 20 times, less on your first time.*
- *On the final breath, end with an inhale, arms raised. Pause with the breath sustained, then exhale through the mouth 3x as you come forward.*
- *Draw the navel to the spine and allow the breath to remain outside.*
- *Allow the body to come to an erect position first, then release the navel and allow the breath to flow in.*
- *Bring the hands into adhi mudrā (thumbs in the palms of the hands, fingers wrapped around the thumbs) and bring the knuckles to rest on the thighs.*
  - o *Inhale to 2/3rds capacity and retain the breath.*
- *When you need to release, all the hands to open and the breath to flow.*
  - o *Sense into your hands. Sense the left cheek and the right cheek. Sense the tip of the nose. Perhaps the cobwebs have cleared and there is a little more energy present.*
- *Practice up to two more rounds of 20 – 25 breaths each.*
- *This breath will temporarily elevate BP, but upon completion, BP is generally lower than the original resting rate. If you feel dizzy or agitated after practice, only practice one round.*
- ***Bhastrikā should be done in a seated position only, as it may cause you to***

Adhi Mudrā

become lightheaded.
- *Practice in the morning to wake up, but not after 2pm. This practice could keep you from going to sleep at night.*
- *Contraindications: high states of anxiety, unmedicated high blood pressure, pregnancy (2nd trimester on), bi-polar with a tendency towards mania, and recent head injuries.*

Self-Inquiry Questions/Writing Prompts:
- How did you like this breathing practice?
- What does your energy feel like after this practice?
- Did you experience a change in your mood?

Practice to Energize

Now you may be ready to come to standing. You might be ready for exercise or an on the mat yoga practice. The important part is that you are up and standing. This might be an excellent time to do some standing breathing practices to help cultivate your energy and clear your space. You need to get up to go to the bathroom, why not try a breathing practice?

Experience: Pulling Prāna and Breath to Stimulate the Nerves

This practice is done standing and is an excellent alternative to bellows breath. The chance of getting dizzy is less because the knees are bending during the course of the breath. This practice is followed by Breath to Stimulate the Nerves, which is a breath retention. When we do rapid breathing practices a breath retention is important to help balance the blood gases.
- *Come to a standing position.*
- *Inhale and swing the arms up over the head, with the hands open, palms facing up.*

- *On the exhale, close the hands, bend the knees as you sweep the arms down and back behind you imagining that you are drawing the energy of your bhāvanā through you. Practice 10 times.*

- *Switch to bringing the arms out in front of you as you inhale.*

  o *On the exhale, bend the knees as you bring the arms behind you, drawing the energy of your bhāvanā through you. Practice 10 times*
- *Switch to alternating the arms as though you are cross country skiing, making sure to bend the knees as you move from side to side. Practice 10 times.*

- *Release and sense the left palm, sense the right palm.*
- *Moving into Breath to Stimulate the Nerves, inhale the arms in front, make fists, sustain the breath as while pumping the arms.*
  - *Arms are bent at the sides and the pump is a movement forward and back of about six inches. Use a medium speed to pump.*
- *Listen to your body and when you need to inhale, release the arms, and stand with palms open.*
- *Sense the palms of the hands, the shoulders, the face, the tip of the nose. Feel the breath moving in the body, perhaps the energy is a little more awake.*
- *Video of Pulling Prana: https://youtu.be/IMqy-CSKk7U*

Self-Inquiry Questions/Writing Prompts:

- How did you like this practice?
- What does your energy feel like after this practice?
- Did you experience a change in your mood?

Experience: Breath of Joy

This breath does not create joy, or bring joy, rather it clears the space for the free flow of joy. Breath of Joy is similar to Pulling Prāna in that it is an energizing breath done standing, which means that the knees are bending when you swing your arms. In the 1970s, Lila Ostermann shared Breath of Joy with hundreds of teachers at Kripalu and it has become a part of the Kripalu tradition. It is also a part of the LifeForce Yoga tradition, although we have adapted it to accommodate for back issues as well as added sound. Breath of Joy is a three-part inhale that helps you fill your lungs and an exhale with the sound lam (pronounced lum) to help you ground and release.

- *Make sure that you have enough space to open your arms wide without hitting anything.*
  - *If you have shoulder issues, feel free to adjust by not moving your arms as much.*
- *Inhale one third of the breath bringing the arms in front of you.*

- *Inhale the second third of the breath bringing the arms out to the side.*

- *Inhale the final third of the breath bringing the arms up over the head.*

- *On the exhale, using the sound lam, bring the arms down alongside the torso as you bend the knees and reach the hips behind you as in a chair pose.*

- *Practice 10 to 15 breaths.*
- *When you finish, allow the palms to rest open at your sides as you sense into the fingers, the palms, the left cheek, and the right cheek. Notice where you feel the most movement of energy or*

breath in your body. Perhaps you feel more awake, more present, maybe even more joyful.

- *Please note, one of the side effects of breath of joy can be smiling.*

Use Breath of Joy for a midday break when you need to get some energy moving. This breath is an excellent practice for Seasonal Affective Disorder, practice it when you are feeling low and missing the sun in winter.

Summary

To lift the heaviness of tamas, the body and mind need to move. Start with where you are, honoring that lethargic state; there is a good reason for why your energy is heavy. Begin with slow and gentle movements in a supine position, lying in bed, on the floor, on the couch, or wherever you are. Once the energy is moving a little, you can begin to move into an upright position and even some stronger breathing practices.

FINDING THE DIMMER SWITCH
TOOLS FOR CALMING

I am feeling strange. There is an elephant sitting on my chest and I cannot find my breath. My vision is beginning to tunnel and I am dripping sweat. My husband and I are in the middle of moving and I am stressing out over every little detail and penny. I have to get out of here. He takes one look at me and tells me to take a break. As I turn around, the panic overwhelms me. Helpless, I bend over, put my hands on my knees, open my mouth wide and start taking gulping breaths while tears stream down my face.

My Inner Self whispers, "Rose, get moving, you have to move." Even though I cannot seem to breathe, I start walking, crying, and chanting "I can't do this. I can't do this." I know this mantra is not helping, but I need to express and purge those helpless feelings. I have never moved across the country to an unknown place before. I am frightened, excited, and overwhelmed, all at the same time.

I keep wanting to stop and gulp the air, but I am also coming back to myself. Walking, chanting, and crying. "I can do this," I say to myself, "this is a panic attack, I know how to work with this." I focus on the feeling of my feet moving and look to the end of the block. When I make it there, I turn around to walk to the other end of the block. My chant starts to change to, "I can make it through today. I can make it through today." As I am saying this out loud, I slow it down, speaking slow and soft to myself. My breath and heartbeat are slowing, and the tears are changing from frantic to releasing.

"Rose, you can do this. You have support. If you need to take another day, you can. None of this is worth your health. You can do this. You got this!" When it comes down to it, I trust myself and I know how to talk to myself in a supportive way. This was not always the case, but it is now. I stop at the end of the block and now I am taking slow deep breaths through my nose. My eyes are closed, and I welcome feelings of calm and ease. I breathe forgiveness and love through my whole body. I am ready to get back to the task at hand.

All told, this incident lasted maybe 10 minutes. It was intense and overwhelming. The aspect that I most want to highlight is that I let it happen. I had all these feelings building up inside me and they exploded. When I gave myself permission to feel and acknowledge the overwhelm, anxiety, and seeming endlessness of moving, things began to flow through me. I kept myself moving through the process, using up some of the energy that was threatening to bowl me over. If I had been sitting down, I do not think that I could have gotten through the panic.

Controlled Burns and Fire Lines

This is rajasic energy. It is light and it can burn like a fire and run like a freight train. We need that rajasic energy to get up and move around, but at the end of the day, it can still be running, and we are at its mercy. We need to let some of that rajas burn off, and yet we set up fire lines, so it does not burn too much, or set the rest of our energy on fire.

When I was in my twenties, I went to be a nanny for my cousin. We were in a remote area of Southwest New Mexico. My cousin was running a large ranch and was working on fire management. Instead of doing small controlled burns, he shared that the best thing was to create fire lines during the wet season around where they wanted to burn and then in the winter set fire to desired area and let the fire burn itself out. Mother Nature knows how to take care of herself. Wildfires are supposed to burn fast, taking the underbrush and dead things, while leaving the larger growth. When people become involved, fires are always put out, and now we have fires that burn slow and hot, destroying areas to a point where it will take decades for them to come back. On a sunny day in January, I got to watch as a helicopter came in and shot napalm into the area slated to burn. All that day my cousin and his crew monitored the fire line. In the morning, the fire was out. Mother Nature and people working together.

Rajas is like fire. When it is tamped down and forced into a corner, it can get out of control. We have to let rajas move. And we have to set limits. A rajasic person going to an intense yoga class to burn some energy off can get carried away. This person goes to the Hot Yoga class, does the practice, and leaves before the rest at the end. They go to work, and we can only imagine how intense this person is at work. Then they go to the gym for a hard core work out at the end of the day. This fire has jumped the road and is consuming everything in its path.

Rajas needs to experience itself and get some of the calming, cooling, and grounding practices. This is just like tamas, in terms of meeting the mood. Rajas differs from tamas in the same way that the night is different from the day. Think about the differences in yourself from day to night, like hormones, emotions, thoughts, digestion, and more. It is the same with rajas and tamas. The aforementioned change from a rajasic state to a tamasic state. Depression and anxiety might go hand in hand, but they are different, and we need to honor those differences.

The best guideline with rajas is to give it space and room to move, within reason. Then we start the calming and grounding of the energy. The exact formula is different for each person and varies from day to day. One way to know is to experience a practice and then pause to explore the aftereffects of the practice. If the mind jolts out of the experience, you likely need more movement. If you are able to focus for a few moments, you may be ready to move to calming and grounding practices. The more you play with this experience, the more you will be able to hear the messages from your body and energy.

The practices in this chapter differ from the energizing practices in the last chapter, mostly to give you a variety of practices. You could burn off the energy with Bellows Breath, Pulling Prāna, or Breath of Joy. The next time you feel you have too much energy, you could try one of those practices, especially it resonates. You could also use Bouncing and Power Hara as energizing practices. There is no set way to do the practices in LifeForce Yoga, there is a toolbox to support you in building the best pathway to inner radiance.

Bouncing

This is my favorite practice! One LifeForce Yoga Practitioner called it "Ants in the Pants," and that is a perfect way to describe what we are doing. Get those ants out of your pants. Once they are gone, everything is easier. The other reason I love this practice is that it helps me get those steps in. When I am short on my steps, 10 minutes of bouncing will get that number up.

Yogis have done dynamic moving and shaking for thousands of years. In my experience, many people find the dynamic version of shaking all the parts of the body at the same time to be akin to lunacy. I have a hard time getting the group to join me in what looks like running from a swarm of bees. The more structured bouncing, taught to me by Dr. Richard Brown, is gentle and accessible.

Shaking is one of the best ways to let go of irritations, aggravations, emotions, tensions, triggers, and traumas. Animals allow themselves to shake after they have experienced something intense. And even though we are animals, humans are always shutting down this natural experience of letting go. Some people, like Peter Levine and David Berceli, have built their work around this process of letting go.

Bouncing also helps to release the lymph. Your lymphatic system is your immune system and your interstitial fluid. It carries nutrients from the blood to the cells and garbage from the cells to the blood. But your lymph has no pump. It relies on deep breathing and movement to circulate. If you have ever had swollen feet or ankles after getting off a plane, that is your lymph collecting in the feet. Our emotions/thoughts float around in our lymphatic fluid. After a time, hours to days, if those emotions/thoughts are not released, they get stored in the body. Where we store these emotions/thoughts is different for each person. If you have a place in the body where you tend to experience a lot of tension, it is a pretty good bet that you are storing your emotions/thoughts there.

Experience: Shake It Off – The Practice of Bouncing

- *Stand with your feet flat on the ground and hip distance apart.*
- *Begin to bounce by bending at the knees.*
  - *Make sure that your feet remain connected to the floor the whole time, otherwise you will create even tighter calf muscles.*
- *Relax as much as possible, letting the thigh muscles do the bulk of the work.*
  - *If you want to release through the lymph, things need to be relaxed. The more you engage your muscles, the more it stops this process.*
  - *If your thighs need a break, come up on to your tip toes for a couple of bounces.*
  - *You may also wish to raise your arms above the head for a couple of breaths.*
- *Find an easy rhythm, not too fast and not too slow. You may have spent a lot of time firming things up in your body. Let that go, the point here is to get a good jiggle going.*
- *Make sure that you are taking deep breaths in and out through the nostrils.*
- *Try for 10 minutes. In the beginning, you may wish to start with two minutes and work your way up.*
- *As you near the end of the practice, take six deep full breaths, sighing it out on the exhale.*
- *When you finish your sixth breath:*
  - *Stand on one leg and shake the other out like a dog getting scratched behind the ear. Then switch legs.*
  - *With both feet on the ground, shake your knees like a frightened cartoon character.*
  - *Move the shake to your hips like Shakira, the Columbian musician and belly dancer.*
  - *Take a big breath in, hold it for a moment, and let your belly shake like a bowl full of jelly. Then let the breath go.*
  - *Move the shaking to your shoulders as you shimmy, shimmy, shimmy.*
  - *Bring the arms over head and shake them in the air like Kermit the Frog.*
  - *Now shake everything. Shake, shake, shake. Moving all the body parts all at the same time. Let it all go.*
- *Come to stillness and let the eyes be soft.*
  - *Feel the left palm and fingers, the right palm and fingers.*
  - *You might notice lots of tingling in the hands. Maybe you are even aware of the current of energy flowing under the skin.*
- *Inhale the breath and energy up to the crown of the head and mentally say "I am"*
- *Exhale the breath and energy through the body to the soles of the feet and mentally say, "here," or "grounded," or some other power word.*
- *Repeat the breath moving in the body four more times.*
- *When you are ready, all the eyes to open.*
- *Watch a video of this practice: yogafordepression.com/bouncing*
- *Cautions: empty your bladder before beginning; if you have edema in the limbs, practice with*

caution; if the knees hurt, switch to a chair and focus on shaking the arms.

Self-Inquiry Questions/Writing Prompts:

- How did this practice land for you?
- What did you notice in your limbs, the hands and the feet, after the practice?

Power Hara

The hara is the Japanese term for the solar plexus chakra, or energy center. This practice is about waking up this center of personal power, self-esteem, and boundaries. Power Hara can help to release energy and pent up anger. This is a two-part inhale and a two-part exhale with a twisting action. You will be inhaling half of the breath, then a quick pause as you rotate to the other side to inhale the rest of the breath. On the exhale we use the sound of "ram" (pronounced rum) twice. There can be limitations in some bodies for this practice, but anyone can do this, as long as you start slow.

Experience: Waking Up the Power Center

- *Stand with the feet wider than hip distance apart, toes pointed out, and arms extended.*
- *Bring the tips of the fingers to the shoulders keeping the elbows wide.*
- *Inhale ½ of the breath to the left, ½ of the breath to the right, keeping the elbows bent.*

- *Exhale with "ram" to the left, extending the right arm across the body, "ram" to the right, extending the left arm across the body.*

- *For SI Joint, low back, and knee protection allow the hips to rotate with the shoulders. If you start to feel dizzy, or too much, slow the practice down.*
- *Practice 10 – 15 times.*
- *When you complete, release the arms, and stand with the palms open.*
- *Sense into your left palm, fingers, forearm, and shoulder. Sense your right palm, fingers, forearm, and shoulder. Notice if there is a little more warmth in the body. Even an internal sense of strength.*
- *If you feel the need to ground this energy:*
  - *Inhale the breath and energy up to the crown of the head and mentally say "I am"*
  - *Exhale the breath and energy through the body to the soles of the feet and mentally say, "here," or "grounded," or some other power word.*
  - *Repeat the breath moving in the body four more times.*

Self-Inquiry Questions/Writing Prompts:

- How did this practice land for you?
- Do you feel a sense of warm in the abdomen?
- Did you experience a sense of release?

Calming Mantras to Add to Movements and Meditations

Sound is one of the best ways to calm the energy of rajas. The longer you exhale the more the calm response in the brain becomes stimulated. I sometimes wonder if I could exhale my way into enlightenment. Add sound to those exhales and the vibrations move through the nervous system inviting even more calm and ease.

The sounds that work best for calming are the releasing chakra tones. These are the simple vowel sounds that you can add to gentle movements.

- Ō, pronounced oh, is used for the first chakra
- Ū, pronounced ooo is used for the second chakra
- Ah is used for the third chakra

- Ā, pronounced eh, is used for the fourth chakra
- Ē, pronounced eee, is used for the fifth chakra
- M, pronounced mm, is used for the sixth chakra
- Hing is used for the seventh chakra.

Experience: Śavasana with Cooling Mantra

Remember to burn off some energy before trying this practice, otherwise it will not feel good. Sit or lie down on the floor. Support all the parts of you that need support. If your low back is tender, bend the knees bringing the feet to the floor.

- *Allow the eyes to soften.*
- *Bring the awareness to the base of the spine. On the exhale, use the low tone of "oh" to vibrate through the base of the spine and legs. Do this one more time, imagining that the sound is coming from the root chakra.*
- *Bring the awareness to the lower abdomen. On the exhale, use the low tone of "ooo" to vibrate through the lower abdomen and low back. Do this one more time, imagining that the sound is coming from the sacral chakra.*
- *Bring the awareness to the upper abdomen. On the exhale, use the low tome of "ah" to vibrate through the upper abdomen and mid back. Do this one more time, imagining that the sound is coming from the solar plexus chakra.*
- *Bring the awareness to the heart center. On the exhale, use the low town of "eh" to vibrate through the heart and upper back. Do this one more time, imagining that the sound is coming from the heart chakra.*
- *Bring the awareness to the throat and neck. On the exhale, use the low tone of "eee" to vibrate through the throat and neck. Do this one more time, imagining that the sound is coming from the*

throat chakra.
- *Bring the awareness to the third eye center at the forehead. On the exhale, use the low tone of "mmm" with the lips touching to vibrate through the brow point. Do this one more time, imagining that the sound is coming from the third eye chakra.*
- *Bring the awareness to the crown of the head. On the exhale, use the low tone of "hing" to vibrate through the crown. Do this one more time, imagining that the sound is coming from the crown chakra.*
- *Using one exhale, roll those seven sounds together. Repeat two more times.*
- *If there is an area that feels like it needs more calming or release, spend some time repeating that sound.*
  - *One way to know if an area needs a little more calming or release is if the sound comes out in a croak.*
- *After several repetitions, allow the sound to fall away as you rest back into relaxation.*
- *Use this practice as a midday rest, at the end of exercise, or as a doorway into sleep at night.*

Other sounds that are calming and can be used in practices like movements, or the Bhāvanā practice are:
- *Om* is the universal mantra that is said to be the sound of creation.
- *So-ham* can be translated to "I am that."
- *Shanti* is the Sanskrit word for peace. When used in mantra practice it is often repeated three times.
- Sha-ma-ya, used to evoke a sense of peace

Self-Inquiry Questions/Writing Prompts:

- How do I know when my energy is calmer?
- What does it feel like to release the excess energy?

Finding the Earth

When it feels as though some of the intensity has softened, it is time to instill a greater sense of calm. This can be done through hand gestures, continued use of sound, movements, meditations, etc. The more we can use the body, the easier it is to ground and center. When the nervous system is beginning to balance, the mind can begin to calm. There are obvious exceptions, like during exercise when the mind slips into that one-pointed focus. In general, forward bends and twists are soothing and calming, which helps to reduce feelings of anxiety.

Experience: Bringing the Energy Down

This is a modified practice that can be done without a yoga mat. I have given the movements their yoga names for those with a yoga practice who want to practice on the mat. You will need a chair for this experience. As you breathe through the nostrils, inhale for a count of four and exhale for a count of six.

Uttānāsana (oo-tahn-ah-sa-na), meaning "intense thinning pose," for its focus on lengthening the spine and sides of the body.

Bring the feet hip distance apart in front of the seat of the chair. If your legs are tight, bring the feet wider. Press your feet into the floor as you imagine the spine lifting up out of the pelvis. With hands on the hips, hinge forward at the hips until you can rest the hands on the seat of the chair without rounding your low back. If you do not have the flexibility to bring your hands to the seat of the chair, use the back of the chair.

Let the tailbone begin to stick up behind you and keep your knees soft. On every inhale, imagine that you could expand your breath into the back of the body. With every exhale, begin to lengthen the spine. Allow the eyes to soften as you release the head. Begin to add the soothing sound of "ahh," drawing it out for as long as you can. Do this three to six times.

Pārśvottānāsana *(parzh-vo-than-ah-sa-na), meaning "intense thinning of the side pose," for the way it continues the work of Uttānāsana in lengthening the torso, yet it focuses that effort on one side only.*

From your forward fold, step your left foot back, angling it out to the side to protect the hips. Allow the forward knee to be soft, even bending it if you need to. Feel free to use the back of the chair for the hands if the legs are tight, it does not help to overstretch the muscles. Begin to add all the soothing sounds, rolling them together like so, "oh-oo-ah-eh-eee-mm-ng." You will notice that the hi from hing disappears when you roll them together. Do this three times. Allow yourself to take three breaths before you do this on the other side.

Once you have completed this on both sides, bring the feet together, to rise up to standing. Allow the eyes to be soft as you notice your feet on the ground. You may feel a rising of energy to the head. Allow the mind to be open to observe all possible feelings, maybe even those of the fluids settling in the body. Notice if you feel a little quieter.

Bālāsana *(ba-la-sa-na), meaning "child's pose," for the way it invites us into the surrender and repose of a child.*

Release yourself to the ground onto all fours. Bring the big toes to touch and the knees wider apart. Inhale here. On the exhale, press your hips back towards your heels, and let the forehead come to the floor. If the head does not touch, stack the hands, use a pillow, or even stack fists on top of each other. Begin to rock the head side to side, rolling across the forehead. Add the sound "mmm," soothing the tired juices in your mind. Do this three to six times.

Jathara Parivartanāsana *meaning "revolved abdominal pose," for the twist that this posture gives to the abdomen and stomach.*

From child's pose, bring yourself to your back. Bend both knees allowing the feet to rest on the floor. Inhale with the knees bent. Exhale and bring both knees to the right. If you wish, stack the knees on top of each other. Rest your right hand on the left knee. Allow the left arm to open to the left with the palm up. On the next exhale roll the calming and soothing sounds together, "oh, oo, ah, eh, ee, mm, ng." Practice the sounds three to six more times. When you are ready, inhale to center. Exhale the knees to the left to repeat the practice on the other side.

When you finish, come back to center. Release the body into shavasana and notice how the breath is moving. Perhaps the mind is calmer and more focused. You may even wish to practice the calming tones again.

Self-Inquiry Questions/Writing Prompts:

- How did that practice land for you?
- Did the mind begin to calm and focus?
- Did you feel the need to hold the positions for longer, or could you have gone with a shorter practice?

Calming Yoga in Your Hands: Mudrās

Pala Mudrā – The Gesture of Calming Anxiety

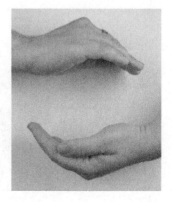

This mudra is named after the bowl that monks use to receive alms in India. The name indicates that this gesture is about receptivity and trust. When we practice this gesture, we are invited to receive and cultivate a trust – in ourselves, our Inner Radiance, Divine essence, our Higher Power.

This mudrā helps to draw the breath into the lower abdomen. Abdominal breathing is soothing and helps to stimulate the parasympathetic nervous system (PNS). When the PNS is stimulated, it shuts off the sympathetic nervous system (fight or flight), which brings about calm and the ability to rest and digest. Anxiety is characterized by spending too much time in the fight or flight zone.

Experience: The Gesture of Calming Anxiety

Come into a position where the spine can belong extended. Cup both hands. Bring the left hand about below the navel with the palm facing up. Bring the right hand to navel level with the palm facing down. Let it be as though you are holding a ball of calm energy between the palms of the hands. Allow the hands to touch the body. Soften the shoulders and any effort from the arms. Allow the eyes to soften as you connect with the thread of your breath.

Feel the breath drawn into the lower abdomen and your energy grounding. Perhaps a sense of releasing any energy that is no longer needed. Support this releasing by using the sounds "oh" and "oo." Combine these two sounds on three exhales. Inhale… "oh…oo." Allow the jaw and the throat to soften. Inhale… "oh…oo." Letting go of whatever it keeps you from feeling grounded and connected to your inner tranquility. One more time. Inhale… "oh…oo."

Out of this radiation of sound, invite an experience of trust. Perhaps it is a moment when you felt trusting of another, or of yourself. Perhaps it is a vision of what trust looks like. If nothing arises, feel free to let it be an intellectual exercise instead. An invitation to dive into this experience of trust. The sense that everything is happening for you. A sense that the entire universe is conspiring for your highest good. Allow yourself to step out of the confines of right and wrong into the expansive experience of trust. Letting go of the need to adjust and to fix, rest into that experience of trusting the universe. Taking three more breaths with this experience.

From this experience of the universe conspiring for you, allow your heartfelt prayer to arise. Let that this seed that the heart is planting for your personal and spiritual growth being nourished by the support of the energy of the universe. Take three more breaths imagining your heartfelt prayer as true and already happening.

When you finish your third breath allow the hands to rest open in the lap. Sense into the palms of the hands, warm or cool. Sense into the breath watching how the breath is flowing. A sense of tranquility, or inner peace, or trust, or security, or any other experience that has arisen for you. When you're ready allow the eyes to open.

Self-Inquiry Question/Writing Prompt:

- What does it feel like to experience a sense of things happening FOR you, instead of to you?

Adhi Mudrā – Gesture of Stillness

Adhi means "first" or "primordial," and it is said to be the first mudrā that humans practice. It connects us with the innate stillness. From that place of stillness, we are able to hear and experience our Inner Radiance. This mudrā activates the earth element – that which is stable, firm, foundation, still, supportive, and even immobile. Adhi Mudrā helps the embodiment practice by activating the parasympathetic nervous system response, which turns off the sympathetic nervous system response. When working with anxiety, hold this mudrā, in your lap, under a table, in your pocket, or anywhere your hands are free to take this position.

This mudrā is the most calming of all the mudrās and may have a sedating effect. During the practice of Adhi Mudrā it is normal to feel the heaviness within the breath, or perhaps even the experience of no breath. When the physical body relaxes, the mind has no choice but to eventually follow. With a regular practice of this mudrā, you may experience a deeper sense of calm on a regular basis. You can use this mudra to help you sleep at night.

Experience: The Gesture of Stillness

For this Mudrā meditation, you may wish to practice in a seated position, or lie flat on the earth. Fold the thumbs into the palms and allow all the other fingers to curl around the thumbs. Turn the fists so that the finger edge of the fist is towards the earth. If you are in a seated position place the fists on the knees and extend the arms so that the elbows straight. If you are lying down, allow the mudra to rest on the floor on either side of you, or resting on your abdomen.

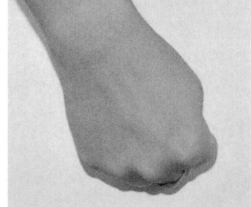

Soften the eyes and allow the breath to flow. Feel the depth of the breath on unfolding into the abdomen. Allow the exhale to lengthen. You may even experience a natural pause at the end of the exhale. Even as the breath seems to deepen, it may also begin to soften and even slow.

Begin to cultivate an experience of stillness. This may be a place in nature, or a feeling of resting into stillness. Imagine yourself in this place of stillness, here and now. Soften any effort that you are using to hold the mudrā. Nourish the seeds of stillness and grounding, using the seed sound for the root chakra "lam." Use this sound four times, on four exhales, placing the emphasis on the L-sound. Allow the sound to be nice and low. Inhale, exhale… "lam." Inhale, exhale… "lam." Allowing the sound to vibrate stillness through the whole body. Two more times. Inhale, exhale… "lam." Inhale, exhale… "lam." As the sound fades, allow yourself to rest into stillness. You may find that the breath becomes almost imperceptible, as though breathing is a chore. Rest into whatever space of no breath you may find yourself.

Every exhale invites a deeper sense of softening. Every exhale invites relaxation. In this experience of growing rest and growing ease, feel that there is more space, more room for your spiritual intention to unfold. Imagine your spiritual intention rising within the stillness. Allow it to be the focal point of your attention.

Release the mudrā. Allow the hands to rest with the palms open. The thumb may still feel encased by the other fingers. Perhaps the center of the palm is warm. Perhaps the mind feels quieter. Perhaps even the space around you is more still. And whenever you are ready, allow the eyes to open.

Self-Inquiry Question/Writing Prompt:

- How do you experience internal stillness?

Calming Prāṇāyāma

The two breaths that follow are great for anxiety, though more challenging to practice in a yoga posture. The best yogic breath is to exhale longer than you inhale, and this can be done in all postures. The breathing practices that follow are more stand-alone practices. You can use them in a seated position or even lying down. I have even used these breaths while driving and on hot days.

Tacos and Tostadas

Śītalī prāṇāyāma (pronounced shee-talee), means "cooling breath." It used to cool the body and mind. We curl the tongue to practice śītalī. You might call this breath "taco shell breathing."

Sītkarī prānāyāma (pronounced seet-karee), means making a hissing sound. It is practiced by drawing the air in through the mouth over the tongue making a hissing sound. An adaptation for accessibility is to draw the breath in through the lips in the shape of a straw. Sucking the breath in with the hissing sound can irritate sensitive teeth. You might call this breath "tostada shell breathing."

Cooling and Calming Breaths

- *Sit in a comfortable position with the spine erect. If you wish, you can come to a supine position— flat on your back.*
- *Open the mouth and form the lips into an "O".*
- *Push the tongue out through the opening so that the edges curl up forming the shape of a leaf about to open.*
    - *If this is not possible, keep the lips in the "O" shape and place the tip of your tongue against the opening.*
- *Draw air in through the tongue slowly as though sipping through a straw.*
- *After a full inhale, draw the tongue into the mouth, gently tuck the chin as you place the tongue on the roof of the mouth and slowly exhale through the nose.*
    - *At the very end of your exhale, wet the tongue by coating it with saliva.*
- *This is one round – continue for 5 minutes.*
- *Feel free to take integrating breaths between each round.*
- *Add a visualization of a cool or cold place, imagining yourself practicing this breath in that place.*
- *Use peppermint in the mouth to aid the cooling process.*
- *You can practice this breath anywhere, anytime. It is excellent for calming anger, if you experience hot flashes, and for migraines.*

Self-Inquiry Question/Writing Prompt

- How do you experience the cooling aspects of the breath?

Turning Inward

Bhrāmarī, meaning "bee," is a breathing practice that extends the exhale using a bee like sound in the back of the throat. To make this sound, the throat contracts into a tiny opening, which releases the breath at a very slow pace. This is release is so slow, that you may find your mind gasping for air before you are finished exhaling. This is the experience of the klesha of abhinivesha, clinging to life. With practice, you will find that you are able to exhale with the sound for an extended period.

Due to the extreme calming nature of this practice, it is excellent for reducing rajas. The sound can be so loud in the head that it obliterates intrusive thoughts and constrictive thought patterns associated with depression and anxiety. Try it when you cannot go to sleep at night. This is also a supportive breath of Attention Deficit Disorder, Attention Deficit and Hyperactive Disorder, Obsessive Compulsive Disorder, and those on the autistic spectrum.

Experience: Bhrāmarī (Bee Breath)

- *Sit in a comfortable position with the spine erect.*
- *Inhale through the nostrils, drawing the root of the tongue to the back of the throat.*
- *Slightly tilt the chin and keep the lips sealed.*
- *On the exhale you will be drawing the back of your tongue to the back of your throat, as though dislodging a popcorn kernel, keeping the throat relaxed*
- *Exhale slowly through the nostrils, making a deep buzzing sound in your throat like a bee. Because the lips are closed, you will not hear the "ZZZ" sound. Instead, you will hear a "swarm" of bees in your throat.*
- *Start with three rounds on the exhale only.*
- *Practice this breath no more than 10 times.*

Mudrās for the Practice of Bee Breath

There several different mudrās that can accompany this breath and support the awareness turning inward. The traditional mudrā for this practice is shanmukhī, meaning "six-openings seal," is used to seal the senses from the outer world. The mudrās can intensify the experience of the breath, which may make it overwhelming in the beginning. In some cases, people with sound sensitivities, or traumatic brain injury, feel disturbed by the intensity of the sound in the head. Go slow and gentle. On the flip side, some people have shared that this practice, with the mudrās, alleviates tinnitus for a period.

Shanmukhī mudrā

- Index fingers point to the brow point.
- Middle fingers cover the eyelids, without pressing on the eyes.
- Ring fingers are at the edge of the nostrils, not touching the nostrils.
- Little fingers are placed at the edge of the lips.
- Thumbs press the outer cartilage, the tragus, near cheekbone into the ear canals.

Helmet mudrā

- Bring the hands to the top of the head.
- Pinky/little fingers meet at the hairline.
- The rest of the fingers spread along the scalp, touching or reaching toward each other.
- Thumbs press the outer cartilage, the tragus, into the ear canals.

Covering the Eyes

- Place the hands over the eyes, keeping the fingers together.
- Thumbs press the outer cartilage, the tragus, into the ear canals.
- Relax the shoulders as you practice.

Self-Inquiry Questions/Writing Prompt

- How did the practice of bee breath land for you?
- How do you experience the awareness turning inwards?

Summary

Rajas is as different from tamas and day is from night. The intensity of the fire of rajas needs to burn off, without burning everything in its path. This takes focus and time to check in with the body, mind, and experience. Once burned off, rajas needs forward bends, long exhales, and introspection to calm and ground. Breathing practices that lengthen the breath, especially when we add sound, help rajas to release.

DESTINATION: BEINGNESS

It is day seven of the training. All week I have been hard at work assisting the training, leading early morning sessions, taking care of behind the scene tasks, teaching practices, and answering questions. At this point, I am exhausted, but I am expected to be present in the early morning guided LifeForce Yoga class and meditation. After receiving the morning practice, I feel rested and focused.

We had just finished chanting The Gāyatrī Mantra and meditation as the sun has risen over the Rincon Mountains of my home in Tucson. This vision of the light coming through while we chanted to the light of illumination has never failed to fill me with wonder and awe. The majesty of the new day spilled across the land, onto my yoga mat, and into my heart. Nature in all her glory.

Amy led us into the LifeForce Yoga Chakra Clearing Meditation, and we practiced one round of bellows breath. After we finished that first round, I came into a natural breath retention, that was more of a cessation of breath. I had exhaled and no breath came back in. My mind got quiet on the exhale and stayed in that still point. I could hear Amy leading a second round of bellows breath, and yet I remained in that place of no breath. There was no need to go further with any practice, I was filled with the peace of beingness.

The practice continued with breath and mantra, and I just sat. My eyes were open, and I breathed the imperceptible breath. There was no effort, no need or desire, just a sitting and witnessing. In the desert, from my seat, a vulture caught in a current of air soared back and forth across my line of vision. The saguaro cacti, bathed in the rising sun, looked like they had shimmering auras of golden light, an effect from the sun behind their spines. A hot air balloon made its lazy way across the hills of the desert below.

Everyone was silent, yet the room breathed with the rise and fall of life. There was the pause and crackle of the sound system, the shifting of a body, the whir of a fan, and the sound of the building adjusting under the rising warmth of the sun. My awareness was open to every nuance of life around me. The feeling of the mat under my legs, the blanket wrapped around my body and unevenly tucked to keep my feet warm. The scratchy feel of the blanket under my arms and its light acrylic smell that has never faded with years of use and washing.

This twenty-five-minute memory is tattooed in my mind. The experience was not meditation, which is the absence of perception. It was pure presence, without judgement, or emotion. This was a gift from my Inner Radiance, reminding me of the importance of being. Through this reminder, I become connected to memories of being throughout my life, my mind unfettered by worry, fear, sadness, or even happiness.

Sitting on the cliff of Second Mesa on the Hopi Reservation with the wind rushing up over the edge light a jet engine as I sit gazing over the desert plane for endless miles. Standing on the Kaibab trail in the Grand Canyon looking up at the canyon's edge and the snow line. Sitting on a massive quartz rock that seemed two stories high in Joyce Kilmer National Forest witnessing the rolling hills covered with trees and mist in the Blue Ridge Mountains. Walking around the corner in the road somewhere in Ireland to see a valley ringed by rocky crags where a herd of sheep is grazing on grass so green that I plopped down on my butt to just watch. Every sunrise and sunset where I went out into nature to watch. Standing on my porch and watching the rain fall. Flying through a thunderstorm on an airplane. All these moments are connected by that same feeling of beingness and peacefulness. And there are so many more — micro moments of looking at a plant, the unconditional love in my sweet doggie's eyes, and macro moments of time spent in nature, sitting for meditation and not getting to meditation but settling into beingness. These moments in my youth are far apart. Once yoga entered my life, these moments increase in quantity and length.

Where is this path taking us?

The ultimate goal of yoga is to still the waves of the mind. When this happens, we realize our union with everything, with purusha (pure spirit). In that union, we know that we have never been separate, that we have always been whole and connected. This experience is without words and defies explanation. We all slip into this experience for quick moments, the practice of yoga helps us to become aware that this moment has happened and increase its frequency; this is a challenge. A dedicated practice brings us to the state of union. For now, it is enough to know that this state exists and is available to us.

While the practices in the book are guiding you down the path of self-realization, the first stop on that path is sattva. Georg Feuerstein defines sattva as the "psychocosmic principle of lucidity or sheer existence devoid of conceptual filters and emotional overlays" (Encyclopedic Dictionary of Yoga, 1990). What a mouthful, which I say with love. This definition says that sattva is the state of pure being, without defining experiences or things and without any emotional reactivity. It is a state without wants, needs, or desires, where we can be fully present to what is.

As mentioned before, it is still a guna, which means it is a constriction. Why is the state of pure being a constriction? Because we can get caught there. Sattva can be a distraction along the path of self-realization. The tools that we are using to cope with stress, depression, anxiety, and trauma, are the same tools that have led yogis to self-realization for thousands of years. Keep practicing, keep inquiring, and the practices will lead you to the ultimate state of union.

Self-Inquiry/Writing Prompt: What does balance/beingness look like for you?

You may not always feel like you are in balance. The Yoga Sūtras say that you could not conceive of a state or experience if the seeds for that were not already present within you. This means that you could not even desire a state of balance if you had not experienced it at some point. If balance or beingness seems like a foreign concept in your life, use the practice of bellows breath to clear your mind, so that you can imagine an experience of balance in your life.

- What does balance mean to you?

- How do I define the experience of beingness?

- The things that bring you to an experience of balance are:

- How does balance and clarity feel in your body?

- Three things that you can do to increase balance, beingness, or clarity in your life are:
    1.

    2.

    3.

Meditation

Meditation is the experience of the mind quieting as we being to connect with our Inner Radiance. My favorite quote on meditation is, "prayer is when you talk to God, meditation is when God talks to you" (author unknown). The process of working through yoga supports and strengthens the mind for meditation. Yet, meditation can seem challenging and next to impossible for some people, especially when stress, depression, anxiety, and trauma are present.

When we are depressed or anxious and we sit in silence, we can make things worse. Some of us spend a lot of time running away from what we are feeling because those feelings are so uncomfortable. A practice of meditation asks us to sit still and be quiet. In that quiet, everything that we have been avoiding can flood to the surface. But this does not mean that we cannot start a practice. Meditation is an advanced practice in yoga for when the mind is a ready. A mind that ruminates, obsesses, or worries all the time is not ready for meditation. That mind will consistently fail at meditation and this can make us feel worse about ourselves. It also explains why some of us struggle so much with the practice.

Meditation sits at the end of a long line of practices in yoga that help to prepare the mind for the silence that is meditation. We will touch on each of these aspects of yoga so that you can see the relationship between them and how yoga works to support optimum mental health. The most important take away is that meditation is something that happens TO you; all you can do is create the conditions for meditation to arise. How long this process takes is unique to the individual.

The Process of Meditation

The Yoga Sūtras of Patanjali lay out a process for achieving meditation. This is known as Ashtanga Yoga. There are many wonderful books and translations of the Yoga Sūtras, including Rama Jyoti Vernon's series called The Gateway to Enlightenment (www.rama.yoga), where you can delve into the text as well as learning how to apply this wisdom to your life.

1. *Yamas* (yah-mas) – support for an ethical relationship with the world.
2. *Niyamas* (nee-yah-mas) – support for an ethical relationship with your mind.
3. *Āsana* (ah-sah-nah) – support for your relationship with your body.
4. *Prānāyāma* (pra-nah-yah-ma) – support for your relationship with your energy.
5. *Pratyāhāra* (prat-ya-har-ah) – support for your relationship with your senses.
6. *Dhāraṇā* (dhar-ah-nah) – your relationship with concentration.
7. *Dhyāna* (dh-yah-na) – your relationship with meditation.
8. *Samādhi* (sah-ma-dhee) – your relationship with absorption.

The *Yamas* – developing an ethical relationship within your community:

1. *Ahimsā* (ah-him-sa) – defined as non-violence, means the practice of kindness and non-

violence in thought, word, and deed, to yourself and others.

2. *Satya* (saht-yah) – defined as truthfulness, means the practice of honesty in our thoughts, speech and actions, and abstaining from abusive words, obscenities, gossip, and ridicule.
3. *Asteya* (ah-stay-yah) – defined as non-stealing/non-coveting, means the practice of giving up the desire for that which does not belong to us.
4. *Aparigraha* (ah-par-ee-grah-ha) – defined as non-hoarding, means the practice of letting go of gathering more than one needs.
5. **Brahmacharya** (bra-ma-char-ya) – defined as abstinence and traditionally interpreted as celibacy. In the modern world, this means the practice of moderation.

Self-Inquiry Questions/Writing Prompts:

- In what ways to you practice kindness, towards yourself and others?
- In what ways do you practice honesty, with yourself and others?
- In what ways do you practice non-stealing, with yourself and others?
- In what ways do you honor that you have enough, with yourself and others?
- . In what ways do you practice moderation, with yourself and others?

The *Niyamas* – developing a devotional and ethical relationship with yourself:

1. *Śauca* (shouw-cha) – defined as purity, means the practice of cleanliness, internally and externally, though diet, breathing, movement, and meditation. This also means a clean environment, in our homes, workspaces, and our planet.
2. *Samtoṣa* (some-toe-sha) – defined as contentment, means the practice of releasing desires, which supports the mind in becoming tranquil and easeful. This happens through diet, breathing, movement, and meditation.
3. *Tapas* (tah-pas) – defined as commitment, means the practice of devoting and committing to a regular practice of breathing, movement, and meditation. Through commitment the mind is trained towards contentment, peace, love, and compassion.
4. *Svādhyāya* (svahd-yah-yah) – defined as self-study and study of the scriptures, means the practice of knowing oneself through honesty and self-inquiry. The reading of sacred texts is included here because these texts reflect overcoming human struggles.
5. *Īśvarapraṇidhāna* (eesh-var-ah-pra-nee-dah-nah) – defined as giving oneself as an instrument of Divine action and love. A more secular understanding of this is acceptance and gratitude.

Self-Inquiry Questions/Writing Prompts:

- How do I practice cleanliness of my external space? In what ways might I increase or add to this practice?
- How do I practice cleanliness o my internal space? In what ways might I increase or add to this practice?
- How do I practice enough is enough?
- What are some ways that I can honor that I am enough and that I have enough?
- What am I committed to?
- I am committing myself to this practice every day:
- How do I practice self-inquiry?
- My favorite sacred text(s) to read is:
- What does acceptance mean to me on a spiritual level and how do I practice it?
- How do I practice gratitude?

Āsana – meaning "to be and to breath and to become one with the eternal cosmic vibration" (Rama Joyti Vernon), is developing a relationship with the body. The body is the home for the mind and stores our experiences and memories. We experience detachment from the body because of pain, disease, trauma, and more. Āsana reconnects us to the body. Traditionally āsana is defined as the seat we take for meditation. Āsana has come to mean all the ways of moving the body in a yoga class. From the definition provided by Rama, āsana means any position where you are being and breathing with the intent of basking in your Inner Radiance. There are three guidelines given in The Yoga Sūtras for the practice of āsana:

1. In any position, become comfortable.
2. Postures and positions are mastered by the relaxation of effort and meditation upon the infinite.
3. When the posture is mastered, the gunas are no longer at play. Meaning when you master any position (through relaxation of effort and meditation upon the infinite), you are not held captive by the swings of energy that are the tamas, rajas, and sattva.

Self-Inquiry questions/writing prompts:

- How do I practice moving my body in a way that I can focus on my breath?
- How do I practice different positions that help me honor and reconnect with my body?

Prānāyāma is our relationship to our energy. It is the practice and regulation of the vital forces within the body. Prānāyāma means to lengthen, expand, and control our life force. The expanse of life can be measured in breaths rather than numbers. When the breath is lengthened and expanded, the nervous system comes into a state of balance, which leads to a state of health. If the nervous system is unbalance, or in stress, the body becomes sick. Through the regular practice of prānāyāma, we bring forth our Inner Radiance in each moment. Prānāyāma is also understood as the gateway to concentration, the first stage of meditation.

Self-Inquiry Questions/Writing Prompts:

- How do I practice lengthening and calming my breath?
- How do I practice regulating my energy?

Pratyāhāra – means to withdraw or to regulate the senses. For most of us, our senses are consumed by the external world. On a spiritual level, this explains why the senses dull with age, they have all be used up (yes, I know, that is not how that works on the physical level, but we are diving into the spiritual). I know that my sense of smell increases in intensity after my yoga practice. We regulate our senses by turning them inwards to sense and experience our inner world. This helps to reduce over stimulation. With the increase in technology, our senses are even more over stimulated than before.

Self-Inquiry Questions/Writing Prompts:

- What happens when I get over stimulated?
- How do I experience my inner voice?
- How do I experience inner vision?
- How do I feel and experience my body, from the inside?

Dhāraṇā – our relationship with our mind. Concentration is the act of fixing the mind on a chosen object and holding it there without distraction. Any time the mind wanders, the will brings the mind back to this object. According the Yoga Sūtras, we start the process of concentration by beginning with the breath. Once we have done some breath work and withdrawn the senses, then the mind is ready for concentration.

Self-Inquiry Questions/Writing Prompts:

- How do I practice concentration?
- How do I feel when I practice concentration on one thing?

Dhyāna – continues our relationship to the mind. It is the uninterrupted flow of concentration where there is no longer separation between the chosen object and the seer. Through this connection to the chosen object the mind becomes illuminated. This is where things begin to get more esoteric and complicated. If you start to feel a little lost, do not worry, I will bring it back around again. When we sit for a meditation practice (after the breathing and the turning the senses inward), we begin with concentration. This could be on a picture, a line of scripture, the breath, a posture, or a mantra. We fix the mind on that image and every time we get distracted; we bring it back to that object. This is the practice of concentration. There comes a point where distraction falls away and it seems as though all that it exists is that object. The entirety of our awareness is focused on the object. Through this intense focus wisdom is revealed about that object. If the object is a light bulb, we understand how the light bulb works. In this state, we begin to become aware of our Inner Radiance, our Divine essence, and we see it as all-pervasive in our life. Yet, we are still aware of a separation. This is the practice of meditation, which is a result of a continued practice of concentration. It is something that happens to you, rather than something that you do.

Self-Inquiry Questions/Writing Prompts:

- How have you experienced meditation as described above?
- How would you know you were having that experience?

Samādhi – continues our relationship to the mind and is defined as absorption. Meditation continues and transforms into absorption when the sense of separation falls away. The mind and intellect cease, perception stops, and the soul remains conscious. Again, this is something that happens to us, rather than something we can do. I once asked Rama Jyoti Vernon how we could know that we were in this state if perception ceases. She said, "when you open your eyes and see that the hand on the clock has moved." This means that we should focus our time and energy on concentration and let the rest arise. This may seem esoteric and out of our reach. The good news is that we are primed for this and experience it on a regular basis, we are just not aware of it.

Self-Inquiry Questions/Writing Prompts:

- Recall a time where you became so absorbed in what you were doing that you lost all awareness of the passage of time.
- Are you aware of an experience where you brought your senses inside your body and became absorbed? This could be during prayer, meditation, a yoga posture, lying down for a yoga nidra practice, etc.

Nādī Shodhana: Cleansing the Energy Channels

Nādī Shodhana, or Alternate Nostril Breathing, is described as the best practice for calming the mind and energy, while preparing us for concentration. It is a balancing technique for the mind and the nervous system and one that many people are drawn to practicing. It is called Alternate Nostril Breathing because the breath is alternated through the nostrils. But, like all things yoga, it is not as simple as that.

A nādī is a channel in the body that energy travels through. There said to be 108 main nādīs and thousands of other nādīs. They are described as hollow tubes which allow for the passage of prāna throughout the body. Shodhana is the act of cleansing these channels of any blockages so that energy can move. There are three nādīs with which we will concern ourselves.

1. *Idā*, meaning "comfort," is the channel to the left side of the spine. It begins on the left side of the first chakra at the tailbone and ends in the left nostril. This nādī is connected with lunar energy and our parasympathetic nervous system. When we stimulate this nādī, by breathing only through the left nostril, we are calm, creative, and maybe even asleep. Overstimulated, we might be tamasic, lethargic, foggy, disconnected, or depressed. If we have a deviated septum and only breathe through the left nostril, this could explain a lifetime of depression. We can use the stimulation of this nādī to bring about a state of calm energy, like when we are anxious.

2. *Pingalā*, meaning "tawny," is the channel to the right side of the spine. It begins on the right side of the first chakra at the tailbone and ends in the left nostril. This nādī is connected with solar energy and our sympathetic nervous system. When we stimulate this nādī, we are energized, logical, and maybe even exercising. Overstimulated, we might be rajasic, frenetic, worried, fearful, or anxious. If we have a deviated septum and only breathe through the right nostril, this could explain a lifetime of anxiety. We can use the stimulation of this nādī to bring about a state of awakened energy, like when we are depressed. In her book <u>Yoga for Depression</u>, Amy Weintraub shares the story of a man named Kevin who had a deviated septum and a lifetime of depression. When he began a practice of right nostril breathing, his depression lifted.

3. *Sushumnā*, meaning "most gracious," is the central channel and runs through the center of the spinal cord. It begins at the center of the tailbone and extends to the crown of the head. When idā and pingalā are cleansed and balanced, we experience balance. Through practice and dedication, we can begin to transcend the polarities of idā and pingalā moving prāna into the sushumnā nādī, which leads to self-realization.

You do not have to remember this to experience the balancing effects of nādī shodhana. I share it with you to give you the understanding of why we practice this breath on a metaphysical level. On a physical level, this practice lowers the heart rate, the blood pressure, increases focus, and brings about a state of balance.

Experience: Alternate Nostril Breathing

- *Sit with the spine erect.*
- *Use Vishnu Mudrā by making a fist of your right hand. Bring the index and middle fingers to the base of the thumb while keeping ring, pinky, and thumb extended.*

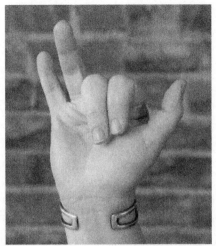

- *Bring the hand in front of the nose. The thumb is for closing the right nostril, the ring and pinky are for closing the left nostril.*
- *Close the right nostril and inhale through the left.*

- *Close the left nostril with the ring and pinky fingers.*
- *Open the right nostril and exhale.*
- *Inhale through your right, then close off the right nostril, then exhale through your left. This is one round.*
- *As you breathe, allow the head to tilt down; this supports the thinking mind to release.*
- *Keep the inhalation even with the exhalation.*
  - *You may also increase the length of the exhale for further stimulation of the relaxation*

response in the brain.

o *There are many ways to adjust the rate of breathing; in the beginning keep it simple.*

- *Always begin and end through the left nostril.*
- *One round = two breaths.*
- *Practice 12 rounds.*
- *If you wish to download a guided practice of Nādī Shodana, head to our website:* *yogafordepression.com/guided-alternate-nostril-breath/*

Tips for practice

- Make sure that the chest is lifting. When the head is lowered, the chest can cave unconsciously.
- Drop the right elbow without squeezing the right arm pit or shoulder.
- The touch of the fingers should be gentle enough to close the nostrils, yet not move the nose from side to side during the practice.
- Concentrate on the gentle movement of the breath in the nostrils and the soft touch of the fingers.
- If you have a deviated septum, place the fingers on the bone of the nose. Air will still move through both nostrils, but the energy and the mind will alternate.

- If one nostril is clogged, use your left hand to draw the flesh of the cheek towards the ear to help manually open the nostril.

Options for practice

- Practice 4 times a day for deep balancing.
- **Left Nostril Breathing** – to calm, for anxiety, or to sleep
  - Option 1: Inhale through the left nostril, exhale through the right. Repeat.
  - Option 2: Inhale and exhale through the left nostril. Caution, this can cause deep relaxation or sleep.
  - Practice a minimum of 12 breaths. If you are using this for sleep, practice until you fall asleep.

- **Right Nostril Breathing** – to energize, for depression, or to awaken
  - Option 1: Inhale through the right nostril, exhale through the left. Inhale right, exhale left.
    - Practice three to six breaths to support digestion.
  - Option 2: Inhale and exhale through the right nostril. Caution, this is very energizing and is considered an advanced practice. Do not use this if you are prone to rajasic states. It is included here for the purposes of providing complete information.

- Add a slight pause of two counts at the top of the inhale.
- Inhale for a count of 4; retain for a count of 16; exhale for a count of 8; pause with

the breath held out for 2. Practice 12 rounds. This is known as *Anuloma Viloma Prāṇayama.*

- o Use practice rounds to build up the ability to hold for longer periods.
- o Use before meditation, before or after yoga practice, and any time you need more equanimity.

An Introduction to the Chakras

Cakra, pronounced chakra (with a hard "ch" sound), means "wheel." For ease of reading, I will use the common spelling of the word, rather than the Sanskrit transliteration. A chakra is a psychic energy center. If you have done some basic exploration into yoga or the metaphysical, you have probably encountered the chakras before. There is a huge compendium of information on the chakras, including some amazing books from Anodea Judith, Wheels of Life, and Nischala Joy Devi, The Namaste Effect. My goal with this basic introduction is to set you up to use the LifeForce Yoga Chakra Clearing Meditation with a basic understanding. If you desire more information, I recommend the aforementioned books.

There are six principle chakras, with the seventh being a transcendence of the physical body. The chakra system extends beyond the crown of the head and there are minor chakras elsewhere in the body, like the hands and feet. The chakras have associated glands, sense organs, colors, animals, etc. The descriptions below keep it simple. When we move the body in yoga postures, we affect the energy in these centers in a specific geometric pattern, which is another reason to practice yoga poses.

Kundalinī is an individualized form of the cosmic feminine energy. It is pictured as a snake that sits coiled at the base of the spine. When kundalinī uncoils, or rises towards the crown cakra, one realizes supreme consciousness and the body is flooded with divine nectar. Union of kundalinī shakti (energy/power) with consciousness obliterates the sense of the individual. Much of yoga is to facilitate this process. Kundalinī awakening is said to be unsurpassably blissful. When kundalinī rises prematurely, it can be a psychically painful process. There are some yogis who would say that mood disturbances are a result of the energy awakening and moving before we are ready.

The Seven Center – Main Chakras

The first chakra, *Mūlādhāra* (moo-la-dar-ah) means "root support." Also known as the root chakra. This is the center of grounding, connection to the Earth, the sense of security, and basic needs being met.

- Location: base of the spine
- Color: Red
- Bīja mantra, energizing sound: Lam
- Cooling mantra: "O"
- Element: Earth
- Gland: Adrenals
- Constrictions:
    o Disembodied
    o Disconnection
    o Scarcity, Unsupported
    o Fear, Insecurity
- Energizing Mudrā: Hasta Mudrā 1
    o Bring the hands into fists with the thumbs on the outside.
    o Extend the pinky fingers, hook them together, and use isometric pressure to pull them apart.
    o Bring the mudrā as close to the base of the spine as is comfortable.
    o Make sure there is room between the hands the body.

- Calming Mudrā: Kanishtha Mudrā
  - o Bring the hands into fists with the thumbs on the outside.
  - o Extend the pinky fingers and touch the tips together.
  - o Bring the mudrā as close to the base of the spine as is comfortable.
  - o Make sure there is room between the hands the body.

Self-Inquiry Questions/Writing Prompt:

- Where do I feel disconnected in my life?
- How does ungrounded show up in my life? In my emotions?
- Where can I increase support in my life?

The second chakra, **Svādhisthāna** (sva-dees-tah-na), means "one's own home," or "dwelling place of the self." Also known as the sacral chakra. This is the center of sexuality, sensuality, and creativity.

- Location: sacrum and hypogastric plexus
- Color: Orange
- Bīja mantra: Vam
- Cooling mantra: "U"
- Element: Water
- Gland: Ovaries/Testes
- Constrictions:
    - Blocked, low energy
    - Numb, closed to life
    - Needy, wounded, addicted
    - Isolation, codependence
    - Rigidity, resistance
    - Separation, disease
- Energizing Mudrā: Hasta Mudrā 2
    - Bring the hands into fists with the thumbs on the outside.
    - Extend the ring fingers, hook them together, and use isometric pressure to pull them apart.
    - Bring the mudrā as close to the base of the spine as is comfortable.
    - Make sure there is room between the hands the body.

- Calming Mudrā: Anamika Mudrā
  - Bring the hands into fists with the thumbs on the outside.
  - Extend the ring fingers and touch the tips together.
  - Bring the mudrā as close to the base of the spine as is comfortable.
  - Make sure there is room between the hands the body.

Self-Inquiry Questions/Writing Prompt

- How do I choose to numb out?
- How do I feel about how I express my sexuality?
- What are my creative outlets?
- How connected am I to my emotions and do I express them?

The third chakra, *Manipura* (ma-nee-pour-ah) means "land of lustrous gems," or "treasure house of the devotee." Also known as the solar plexus chakra. This is the center of self-esteem, strength, courage, power, and knowing your place in the world.

- Location: solar plexus, navel to base of ribs, epigastric plexus
- Color: Yellow
- Bīja mantra: Ram
- Cooling mantra: "Ah"
- Element: Fire
- Gland: Adrenals, pancreas

- Constrictions:
  - Separation, self-interest (constrictive ego)
  - Low self-esteem
  - Lack of clarity
  - Competition, control, power
  - Giving up
  - Imbalance, stress
  - Judgmental, critical, prejudiced
  - Lack of deep values
  - Short-sighted, exploitation
  - Inner & outer conflict
- Energizing Mudrā: Hasta Mudrā 3
  - Bring the hands into fists with the thumbs on the outside.
  - Extend the middle fingers, hook them together, and use isometric pressure to pull them apart.
  - Bring the mudrā as close to the base of the spine as is comfortable.
  - Make sure there is room between the hands the body.

- Calming Mudrā: Madhyama Mudrā
  - Bring the hands into fists with the thumbs on the outside.
  - Extend the middle fingers and touch the tips together.
  - Bring the mudrā as close to the base of the spine as is comfortable.
  - Make sure there is room between the hands the body.

Self-Inquiry Questions/Writing Prompts:

- What makes me feel courageous?
- Do I get caught up in competition/comparisons? If so, how does that make me feel?
- How do I cultivate self-esteem?
- What do I do to express my strength that does not trample others?

The fourth chakra, **_Anāhata_** (ah-nah-ha-tah) means "unstruck sound." Also known as the heart chakra. This is the center of love, compassion, and forgiveness.

- Location: heart, cardiac plexus
- Color: Green
- Bīja mantra: Yam
- Cooling mantra: "Eh"
- Element: Air
- Gland: Thymus
- Constrictions:
  - Distrust
  - Not seeing the gift
  - Blame, resentment, guilt
  - Self-righteousness, judgment
  - Miserly, harshness, sharpness

- o Isolation, loneliness
- o Taking life too seriously
- o Unclaimed treasure
- o Sadness, heaviness
- o Dullness, boredom, monotony
- o Worry, anxiety, troubled heart
- o Separation
- Energizing and Calming Mudrā: Kapota Mudrā
  - o Bring the hands into prayer mudrā at the heart.
  - o Draw the centers of the palms away from each other, as though you are holding something precious in your hands.
  - o Tip the thumbs to the breastbone, making contact.

Self-Inquiry Questions/Writing Prompts:

- What weighs heavy on my heart?
- How do I practice self-love and self-compassion?
- What do I need to accept love from others?
- How can I increase love and compassion in my life?

The fifth chakra, **_Vishuddha_** (vi-shoe-dah) means "pure." Also known as the throat chakra. This is the center of communication, listening, and knowing your truth/your spiritual path.

- Location: throat, carotid plexus
- Color: Blue
- Bīja mantra: Ham
- Cooling mantra: "Ee"

- Element: Space/Ether
- Gland: Thyroid, parathyroid
- Constrictions:
    - Lack of self-awareness
    - Unfocused, undisciplined, many focuses
    - Unquestioned belief patterns
    - I am the conditioned personality
    - No clear path
    - Guided by the logic of the ego
    - Life in the past and future
    - Consumerism
    - Reactivity
    - Clinging
    - Inadequate, incomplete
    - Sense of limitation
    - Doubt, confusion
    - Inner dialogue/doubt
    - Hopelessness
    - Controlling
- Energizing and Calming Mudrā: Padma Mudrā
    - Bring the hands into Kapota (heart chakra) mudrā at the throat.
    - Keeping the thumbs and pinky fingers touching, open the middle three fingers.
    - The thumbs are hovering in front of the throat, but not touching.

Self-Inquiry Questions/Writing Prompts:

- How do I speak up for myself?
- How do I express listening/how do I show others that I hear them?
- What is my spiritual path in life?

The sixth chakra, *Ājnā* (ah-j-na) means "command," "authority," or "unlimited power." Also known as the third eye chakra, or brow center. This is the center of wisdom, intuition, and inner knowing.

- Location: third eye center, medulla plexus, pineal plexus
- Color: Purple
- Bīja mantra: Om
- Cooling mantra: "Mm"
- Element: Soul
- Gland: Pituitary
- Constrictions:
  - Duality
  - Incomplete
- Energizing Mudrā: Kali Mudrā
  - Interlace the fingers so that the right thumb is on top of the left.
  - Extend the index fingers and bring the palms away from each other about an inch.
  - Bring the mudrā in front of the forehead, without touching.

- Calming Mudrā: Anjali Mudrā
    o Bring the hands into prayer position.
    o Touch the thumbs to the brow point.

Self-Inquiry Questions/Writing Prompts:

- In what ways do I feel connected to my inner wisdom?
- How well do I trust and follow my intuition?
- What practices can I add to my day to increase my inner knowing?

The seventh chakra, **Sahasrāra** (sa-has-ra-ra), means "thousand-petaled," or "empty." Also known as the crown chakra. This is the center of our connection to Divine energy.

- Location: top of the head, cerebral plexus
- Color: White
- Bīja mantra: Ng
- Cooling mantra: "hing"
- Element: Spirit (paramatma)
- Gland: Pineal
- Constrictions:
    o Ignorance/the mistaken belief of separation
- Energizing Mudrā: Kali Mudrā
    o Interlace the fingers so that the right thumb is on top of the left.

- o Extend the index fingers and bring the palms away from each other about an inch.
- o Bring the mudrā in front of the forehead, without touching.

- • Calming Mudrā: Dhyāna Mudrā
    - o Bring the left hand into the lap with the palm facing up.
    - o Place the back of the right hand on the left the palm.
    - o Touch the tips of the thumbs together.
    - o Relax the shoulders and the arms.

Self-Inquiry Questions/Writing Prompts

- What does The Divine mean to me?
- What practices do I engage in to connect with the divine?

To help you keep this information straight, here is a graphic:

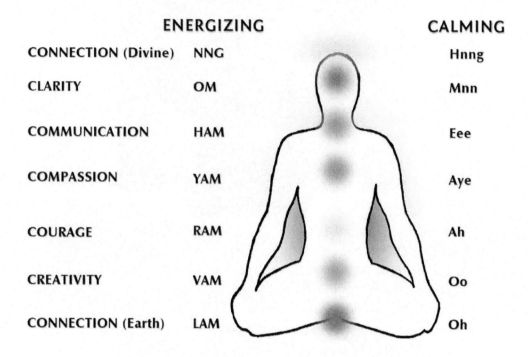

ENERGIZING		CALMING
CONNECTION (Divine)	NNG	Hnng
CLARITY	OM	Mnn
COMMUNICATION	HAM	Eee
COMPASSION	YAM	Aye
COURAGE	RAM	Ah
CREATIVITY	VAM	Oo
CONNECTION (Earth)	LAM	Oh

LifeForce Yoga Chakra Clearing Meditation

The reason that people give up on a meditation practice, despite knowing the benefits of the practice, is that it is difficult. When sitting for meditation, the mind wanders, it gets distracted, and even begins to think of many excuses to now practice. Amy Weintraub created the LifeForce Yoga Chakra Clearing Meditation (LFYCCM) to give the mind a bone in preparation for coming to a state of readiness for meditation. This practice is excellent for everyone. Once you know the practice, you can use it to prepare yourself for sitting for meditation every day.

It combines two breathing practices with mudrās and mantras. There are two different versions of the LFYCCM, one that is meant to energize and one that is meant to calm.

Energizing/Grounding version:

1. Practice 1 – 3 rounds of Bellows Breath (Bhastrikā) to clear the mental and emotional space. 1 round = 20-25 breaths.

2. Practice 3 Bee Breaths (Brāhmarī) using the shanmukhī mudrā, or any of the other options, to help turn the senses inwards.

3. Practice the energizing mantras in a low meditative tone, placing the emphasis on the consonant as you hold the mudrā for each chakra. If you wish, you can visualize the color associated with the chakra.

4. Lift arms over head, creating an open channel, or modify with cactus arms, or arms in the lap. Roll all seven energizing tones together on one exhale. Repeat two more times.

5. Inhale arms over head and bring the hands into kali mudrā. Retain the breath for as long as feels comfortable.

6. Exhale with the "ng" sound, floating your arms down, palms open on your knees.

7. Upon completion, remain in your seated position, and allow the mind to rest in any stillness that has arisen. Rest the awareness on the experience, a breath, or a mantra.

Bellows Breath (Bhastrikā):

Exhale   **Inhale**

Bee Breath (Brāhmarī):

Shanmukhī Mudrā

Mudras for the Energizing Version

Chakra	Mantra	Color	Mudra	
Root Chakra	Lam	Red	Hasta Mudrā 1 Link the pinky fingers together as close to the base of the spine as possible. Pull with isometric pressure.	
Sacral Chakra	Vam	Orange	Hasta Mudrā 2 Link the ring fingers together as close to the base of the spine as possible. Pull with isometric pressure.	
Solar Plexus Chakra	Ram	Yellow	Hasta Mudrā 3 Link the middle fingers together as close to the base of the spine as possible. Pull with isometric pressure.	
Heart Chakra	Yam	Green	Kapota Mudrā Palms together as in prayer. Draw the palms away from each other keeping the outsides of the hands touching. Thumbs touch the breastbone.	
Throat Chakra	Ham	Blue	Padma Mudrā Bring the hands together as in prayer. Keep the base of the palms, the little fingers and the thumbs together. Open all the other fingers wide like petals.	
Third Eye Chakra	Om	Violet	Kali Mudrā Interlace the fingers with the right thumb on top and extend the index fingers. Cup the palms and place the mudrā in front of the forehead without touching.	
Crown Chakra	Ng	White	Kali Mudrā Interlace the fingers with the right thumb on top and extend the index fingers. Cup the palms and place the mudrā in over the crown of the head.	

Calming version:

1. One round of Bellows Breath to meet agitation and burn the energy off. If it feels like Bellow Breath might further agitate the mind, skip over this portion of the practice.

2. Practice 3 Bee Breaths (Brāhmarī) using the shanmukhī mudrā, or any of the other options, to help turn the senses inwards.

3. Practice the cooling and calming mantras with the mudrās. Allow the sounds to be long and drawn out in a low tone. As you roll the sounds together, the "hi" from "hing" will disappear.

4. Keep hands in dhyāna mudrā in lap and roll all seven calming sounds together on one exhale. Practice two more times. and Practice 3x, using one long breath to chant through all the tones.

5. Upon completion, remain in your seated position, and allow the mind to rest in any stillness that has arisen. You may wish to anchor the awareness on the breath, on a mantra, or allow yourself to bask in the experience.

Bellows Breath (Bhastrikā):

Exhale   **Inhale**

Bee Breath (Brāhmarī):

Shanmukhī Mudrā

Mudras for the Calming Version

Chakra	Mantra	Mudrā	
Root Chakra	Oh	Kanishtha Mudrā Touch the tips of the pinky fingers together as close to the base of the spine as possible.	
Sacral Chakra	Oo	Anamika Mudrā Touch the tips of the ring fingers together as close to the base of the spine as possible.	
Solar Plexus Chakra	Ah	Madhyama Mudrā Touch the tips of the middle fingers together as close to the base of the spine as possible.	
Heart Chakra	Aye	Kapota Mudrā Palms together as in prayer. Draw the palms away from each other keeping the outsides of the hands touching. Thumbs touch the breastbone.	
Throat Chakra	Ee	Padma Mudrā Bring the hands together as in prayer. Keep the base of the palms, the little fingers and the thumbs together. Open all the other fingers wide like petals.	
Third Eye Chakra	Mm	Anjali Mudrā Bring the palms into prayer position at the forehead with the thumbs touching the brow point.	
Crown Chakra	Hing	Dhyāna Mudrā Place the right hand on top of the left, with the palms facing up. Touch the tips of the thumbs together and allow the mudrā to rest in the lap.	

Self-Inquiry Questions/Writing Prompts:

- Which version of the LFYCCM did you practice?

- Were you able to sit in stillness at the end of the practice with more ease?

- Did the mind wander more or less than usual?

- How do you experience your Inner Radiance when you create space and silence for the connection to arise?

Summary

The first stop on the road to self-realization and ultimate freedom is sattva, the experience of being. Meditation practices bring allow us to rest in the connection with our Inner Radiance, but we can only get there when we have cleared enough space to pause. The Yoga Sūtras of Patañjali outline a pathway that supports mental health and wellness. When we follow this prescription for behavior and practice, we will arrive at the destination of connection.

FINDING YOUR CENTER
TRAUMA

It was a clear and warm November day in Tucson. I was running late for class because I had to go back into the house to get something. I had gone through the yellow light at the nick of time, but when I saw the next yellow light at a pedestrian crossing, I decided to slow down, even though it might make me later. As I sat at the light, calm, I watched the young woman step off the curb. The next thing I remember was feeling confused and hearing the echo of a loud bang in my mind.

"I think someone just had a car accident," I thought. "Wait, I think it was me." And then I burst into tears, panicking as I looked for the pedestrian, sure that she was lying dead in the street, crushed by my car. She was standing on the other side of the street talking on her cell phone. As I became more aware, my head was pounding and my neck felt tight, weird, and all wrong. Given my training and work with trauma, I knew that I had a head injury, trauma, and that I may be in shock. I declined the paramedics because I wanted to see someone who knew me and who was an expert in car accidents, my chiropractor. Plus, the accident had happened between a church (where I went to Junior High School) and the hospital. If I felt I needed to go, I would walk across the street. Some days I think it was a mistake not to go, others I do not.

I felt weak inside and I kept trying to stabilize my nervous system in the hopes that I could control my trauma response. We moved our now totaled cars, called the people we needed to call, exchanged information, and the usual. All told, that took more than an hour. Then I drove my car of 12 years home. I kept crying about the pedestrian, whose life had been spared, and crying about my car, we were supposed to drive 300,000 miles together. I saw the chiropractor and then a lawyer. Eventually, I would have a number of MRIs and so many appointments that I thought I had gotten a part-time job seeing doctors.

I had to cancel classes and take care of business items, but I could barely think. I knew that I had a concussion, that a neurologist diagnosed as a severe traumatic brain injury (TBI). I also knew that I was high risk for post-traumatic stress disorder. I had been retroactively diagnosed with childhood trauma, which made me higher risk for PTSD in this situation. As the weekend wore on, I realized the concussion was worse than I thought. I was having a hard time remembering the right words for things, my head felt cloudy, I could not remember what happened minutes before, and my filter was gone – I started using curse words again after eight years. Everything up to the car accident was clear, even the moments right before, and then there are big swaths of memories that are gone.

The neurologist told me that I was my training would help my healing. With the head injury and the trauma, I knew that my short-term memory was impaired, that I should not look at screens, and that I needed to rest and do nothing. What I did not know was the high cost of having emotions. I would get upset, or angry, and fly off the handle, screaming, yelling, and crying at the same time. My husband called it "going hulk," and it was like uncontrollable rage. I was scared out of my mind when I became emotionally dysregulated like that. When we were able to get me calmed down, my head would be screaming with a headache so intense that I could hardly remember that I was a human. The only think I could do was sleep for a couple of hours.

And then there were the loud noises. Loud bangs would shake me to my core. I remember driving home from an appointment and a road sign banging in the wind. I screamed and began to cry. The worst part was that my back and neck were hurt so bad at this point, that when I got startled, I felt I could not get away. I would yell and cover my head in fear, which made me feel worse because I have never been the person to freeze in the face of danger. I was broken. My husband said, "you left the house excited about your massage that afternoon and you came home broken."

I did not have PTSD, but I was traumatized. I had depression from the head injury, for which the neurologist said I should not take medication. I had a constant headache, that lasted about six months. I could no longer turn my head without getting dizzy, nauseated, and starting to pass out (I will never be able to turn my head all the way in each direction again). My back was in such intense pain that I could not roll over in bed without grabbing the side of the bed and I yelped getting up off the toilet (which continues, but at least it is a silent yelp). My hands were numb, I dropped things, and the lack of dexterity in my fingers made it hard to open bottles and pick things up off the floor. I could not lift my arms above my head without spasms in my neck. This made teaching difficult and a lot of the LifeForce Yoga breathing practices became inaccessible.

The constant through all of this was my yoga practice, but it had to change. I could not do the standing poses that I loved, nor could I do the breathing practices to lift the depression that had settled in (the neurologist was right, that went away). I longed for a shoulder stand into a plow pose, because they are so nourishing and healing for the nervous system. My days of plow are done, and shoulder stand has become legs up the wall. Instead, I found that I could sit for meditation with ease. My brain could only handle a one-pointed focus, so meditation was easy. Finding the position to sit for meditation was the challenge. I did the Joint Freeing Series that I learned from Mukunda Stiles and I did the back breathing that I learned from Rama Jyoti Vernon. Mudrās were my favorite to practice, because they were nourishing and easy. The mantras were a sweet way to experience sound that I found soothing. Best of all was nādī shodhana. I feel that it was one of the things that helped me most and may have prevented me from turning the traumatization into post-traumatic stress disorder.

I know I will never be the same. Our experiences change us. My body, which was feeling pretty good before the accident, feels like it has aged twenty years. But I am so grateful. I am still here, and I get to use this experience to support others going through similar issues. I chose this trauma story to share with you because it is less intense and because the journey was shorter. If it were not for yoga and LifeForce Yoga in particular, the trauma stories from my childhood would still be controlling my life. I never set out to do yoga to help myself heal; the healing was a wonderful gift that came from my practice.

A discussion of trauma can bring up our own traumas. This chapter is not meant to be a comprehensive education on trauma. There are many wonderful and extensive books and programs on the subject from authors like Peter Levine and Dierdre Fay, a LifeForce Yoga Practitioner. Rather, we will focus on a shorter explanation of a yogic perspective on trauma and then move right into LifeForce Yoga practices. Before we start, take a moment to explore what you need to feel at ease.

Self-Inquiry Question/Writing Prompt:

- What do I do to self-soothe?

What is trauma?

Trauma is a biological response to an injury, and/or a disturbing or distressing event that overwhelms a person's coping mechanisms. It is also an injury to the nervous system. Trauma is subjective, not objective, so the way each person responds to a distressing event is unique to that individual. We all experience traumas, but not all of us will be traumatized or experience post-traumatic stress disorder. The reasons for why are still unknown. It takes a medical professional to diagnose PTSD. If you think that you may be suffering from PTSD, make sure that you seek the help of a professional. The practices here can provide support for PTSD, but they are NOT a replacement for medical care. If you are in the care of a medical professional, feel free to bring this book to your next appointment and show them the practices that you find supportive and helpful.

An Understanding the Autonomic Nervous System and the Gunas

The human body is amazing and what we still do not understand is vast. The information below combines common understandings of the nervous system, combined with yogic information, and some polyvagal theory splashed in. I expect that this information will need to be updated as time goes on. Those of you that have done extensive training on trauma, the nervous system, or the body, will have more knowledge. Again, this is not meant to be a deep education, rather it is a basic jumping off point for an understanding of how the LifeForce Yoga practices work against the backdrop of the nervous system in a state of stress and trauma.

The autonomic nervous system (ANS) regulates the function of the internal organs, like heart rate, digestion, unconscious respiration rate, urination, pupillary response (the pupil's response to light), etc. It is also responsible for the fight or flight response. The ANS is divided into three parts, the Sympathetic Nervous System (SNS), the Parasympathetic Nervous System (PNS), and the Enteric Nervous System (ENS). The ANS is informed by the Vagus Nerve, which originates in the brain and is connected to the hypothalamus. The ENS is a neural network that governs the functioning of the gastro-intestinal system. It can operate independent of the ANS and the vagus nerve.

The Biochemical Response to Stress

An event occurs and it is perceived as a threat by the individual and/or the nervous system. This perception is informed by past experiences and the current state of mind and the nervous system. For example, if you are in a state of stress, you are more likely to perceive the event as a threat. That event could be a physical, emotional, or environmental threat. It could also be deadline, someone yelling at you, or even images that recall the memory of a previous trauma or threat. When this happens, the body prepares for harm. Until most recently, the understanding has been that the limbic brain (amygdala) initiates the stress response. Even though I promised no research, I must share this one little piece (I made it this far, so I get a little treat). In 2019, a piece of research came out that may turn this understanding on its head. In mice, the release of stress response hormones only happened when there had been a chemical released by the bones, giving new meaning to the phrase, "I feel it in my bones." Without the release of that chemical, there was no stress response.

The body's preparation for injury includes the heart rate increasing, blood pressure goes up, blood platelets thicken (cholesterol goes up), breathing faster, digestion stopping, and blood flow to the limbs constricting (cold hands and feet). Our cognitive functioning goes offline as well, this is referred to as "flipping your lid" by Dr. Daniel Siegel. Chronic stress means this response is happening on a regular basis and the brain changes to begin to see stress where there is no stress. This is known as Sympathetic Nervous System (SNS) stimulation and the fight or flight response. In Polyvagal Theory, this is the "Danger Zone," where the nervous system is on alert for potential danger. In terms of the yogic system, this is the guna of rajas. It is not an equal correlation because rajas is also the simple state of being awake and interacting with others.

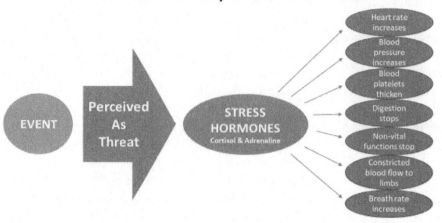

Biochemical Response to Stress

The stress response does not just peter out and turn off. It needs the Parasympathetic Nervous System to activate to turn off. PNS activation known as the "rest and digest" or "feed and breed" system. In polyvagal theory, this corresponds to the "Safe Zone," meaning there have been signifiers that the body/mind/spirit is in a safe place and fight or flight can cease. We are living in a society that is in a PNS deficit. The SNS is activated by so many things, including driving, computer screens, and phones. We need this PNS activation for healing, restoration, and rejuvenation. In terms of the yogic system, this is the guna of sattva.

Sometimes the nervous system perceives a threat that might cause great harm, and the "death-feigning," or freeze response is engaged. According to Polyvagal Theory, this is when trauma happens. In this case, the SNS engagement becomes so intense that the PNS turns on to shut it off. This is when fainting and loss of consciousness happens. In yogic terms, this is the guna of tamas. Using the story of my car accident, my nervous system perceived the impact as a threat to my survival and I lost consciousness. In cases of prolonged trauma, the mind goes elsewhere as a protective measure, called dissociation. In those situations where we may freeze or feel unable to respond, know that the decision made by the nervous system overrides our cognitive functioning.

Experience: Three Deep Breaths

The practice does not have to be complicated to be effective. It can be a simple as three deep breath. Inhale through the nose, pause for a heartbeat or two, and exhale long and slow through the nose. Do this two more times. If you want to increase the calm brain response, use the long drawn out sound of "ah" on the exhale.

A Yogic Perspective of Trauma

All perceptions, sensorial experiences, and actions leave impressions within the subconscious mind (chitta). In yoga, these impressions are called *samskāras*, meaning "activators." These imprints drive conscious and unconscious thoughts into action. It may help to think of samskaras as patterns of behavior. A samskāra could be anything, the way that you brush your teeth, to how you respond to a smile from a stranger, to how you react in a crisis. The Yoga Sūtras state that the mind cannot be changed unless the impressions are brought to the surface where they can be experienced and then transformed or eradicated. This is the process of yoga.

These samskāras form a concentration in the mind called a *vāsanā*, "dwelling." There are said to be countless vāsanās in the mind. These vāsanās make up our unconscious and uncontrollable patterns of behavior and reactivity. There is a loose correlation to epigenetics in the sense that these patterns of reactivity may be built into our DNA as memories and/or changes in gene expression due to the chronic stress in our ancestors. This means that the way we react may be the result of a trauma experienced by an ancestor. Parents may have seen the behavioral patterns of a relative in their child even when the child has not met that relative. But we do not want to go down the rabbit hole of gene expression and epigenetics, which can be quite fascinating. The important take away is that vāsanās determine our perception of an event and whether we will respond with ease or move into a trauma response.

The practice of yoga is to make the invisible visible. Through breathing, posture, meditation, and self-inquiry our unconscious patterns of behavior rise to the surface, where we can let it go. If we practice intense forms of postures and breathing, these samskāras coming to the surface can be painful. When we have a gentle practice, the rising of these samskāras can be gentle and almost imperceptible. It is important to find the practice that works for you.

An Internal Place of Refuge

The Inner Sanctuary is another name for cultivating a bhāvanā of an internal safe space. It is an internal experience of comfort, ease, and peace. It is a resource and coping mechanism to which you can turn to when you feel overwhelmed. The Inner Sanctuary is a place, real or imagined, that when invoked invites a sense of peacefulness, ease, serenity, and even security. This practice is used in LifeForce Yoga Nidra practices and it is a wonderful stand-alone practice.

Experience: Inner Sanctuary

Come into any position and become comfortable. Begin to connect with your inner sanctuary. Your inner sanctuary is that place, real or imagined, where when you go there you feel peaceful, serene, or at ease. This could be a place in nature, a special room, or perhaps a feeling in the body. There might even be beings present that support you and your journey. If more than one place arises, make a composite, an inner sanctuary mural. Imagine yourself in your inner sanctuary right now. With each breath, in your inner sanctuary, feel yourself becoming more peaceful, more serene, more at ease.

As you breathe with your inner sanctuary, notice if there is a feeling of the inner sanctuary within the body. Does the inner sanctuary have a home in your body? Perhaps a sense of ease in the shoulders. Maybe the heart feels a little softer. Perhaps the whole body is feeling a little bit more relaxed. Or an entirely different experience is happening for you. Notice where the inner sanctuary lives in your body. Breathe with it. Fully experiencing the inner sanctuary in your body.

Take in your inner sanctuary through your senses, starting with the sense of smell. Notice smells in your inner sanctuary. If it is outside, perhaps the smell of the forest, or dirt. Perhaps there's a particular scent that permeates the experience of your inner sanctuary. Or maybe there is no smell. Breathe in the smell in as you imagine yourself in your inner sanctuary.

Maybe there are images. Take in the sights, the vision of this sanctuary. Perhaps calming images of nature. Soothing reminders of peacefulness, serenity, or ease. Maybe there is an altar with special and meaningful images. Welcome all that you see or imagine.

Become aware of any sounds in the when you imagine yourself in your inner sanctuary. Maybe there are nature sounds, or even soothing music. Or even the absence of sound.

Notice the ambient temperature on the skin when you imagine yourself in your inner sanctuary. Perhaps it is cool, or warm. Maybe the air is damp, or dry. Notice if there is a breeze, or perhaps the air is still.

There might even be a taste in the mouth when you visit your inner sanctuary. Inviting that taste, moving the tongue in the mouth, and even swallowing.

Welcome the fullness of this experience, that is your inner sanctuary. Feel yourself becoming more peaceful, more serene, and more at ease.

On the next inhale, bring the arms up in front of the heart as though you are holding a ball of energy. Pause and embrace the energy of your Inner Sanctuary. Use the sound of "so-ham" to draw your inner sanctuary to your heart. Let's do that two more times. When you complete, let your hands rest on your heart. This inner sanctuary is on the altar of your heart, available to you whenever you need it.

Self-Inquiry Questions/Writing Prompts:

- My Inner Sanctuary is:
- When I am in my inner sanctuary I feel:

Slowest is Fastest

Patience. Vāsanās are well-worn ruts in our mind and our bodies. A trauma is not just a memory, it also lives in the body. One of the realizations in the field of psychology is that traumas cannot be released if they are only talked about. To release the grip of a trauma, the body must be involved. Peter Levine developed Somatic Experiencing in response to this realization.

The issues are in the tissues. In chapter seven, I talked about the lymphatic tissue and fluid as being a resting place for our experiences. If those experiences are not released, they get deposited into the body. This explains chronic pains in the body that seem to increase with stress. From a yogic perspective, releasing the body will release the samskāras stuck in those tissues. And slowest is fastest!

Rushing through the process of releasing can overwhelm by retraumatizing the tissues and the mind. A gentle yoga practice erodes the issues in the tissues without becoming intense. In my personal experience, practicing yoga for years began to release the grip of my childhood traumas. I did not even notice that it was happening until I began to look back. Life became easier and the things that once triggered me began to have no impact.

Moving slow means using gentle practices and then working your way up to bigger practices. Slow and steady also means that you are more likely to stay with the practice, rather than burn out. The pace at which you move is unique to each individual. Some basic options:

- Grounding practices:
    - Movements that involve the leg muscles.
    - Feeling the feet.
    - Lying down and stretching on the floor.
- Mudrās with mantras:
    - The calming mudrās from chapter seven.
    - The mudrās listed below.
- Slow deep breathing with an emphasis on the exhale.
- Empowerment and embodiment practices:
    - Core engagements, like abdominal workouts.
    - Standing poses like warrior poses.
    - The victory salute (see below).
- Yoga Nidra (see below).

Self-Inquiry Questions/Writing Prompts

- What are the practices that you enjoy that fit into the categories above?
- How can you integrate slowest is fastest as a practice into your life?

A Grounding Breath

In LifeForce Yoga we use Moving the Breath in the Body as a grounding and balancing practice. It is integrated into yoga classes and used after more intense breathing practices. It is a simple breath that can help bring you back to yourself when you feel triggered, anxious, or rajasic. All this practice requires is a little imagination.

Experience: Moving the Breath in the Body

Practice this in any position, eyes open or closed. This helps to balance after any breathing practice, yoga postures, and when every you feel a sense of unease.

- *Inhale the breath through the body to the crown of the head with "I am."*
- *Exhale through the body to the balls of the feet with "here."*
  - *You can also use grounded or any other power word.*
- *Repeat at least five more times, or as long as you need.*

Empowering Yoga in Your Hands: Mudrās

Svasti Mudrā – Gesture of Healthy Boundaries

Svasti means "well-being" and "blessing." Svasti mudrā creates an aura of protection around the body so that one can remain in a state of well-being. The mudrā protects the heart from the negativity of others and environments by crossing the arms. The palms extend the boundary of the field of protection.

Trauma needs healthy and strong boundaries. People with trauma histories struggle with boundaries. That may be because they were in situations where they could not say no. Maybe no one showed them how to say no and establish those boundaries. This mudrā helps us to say no to people and situations that are unhealthy. In turn, this mudrā helps us to say yes to the blessings and well-being of our lives.

Experience: The Gesture of Healthy Boundaries

Come into a seated position allow the spine to be nice and long. Bring the hands into prayer position at the heart. Cross the forearms, bringing the hands in front of the shoulders and the right arm is closer to the chest and the backs of the hands face each other. Allow the hands to be strong with flat palms and the fingers pointed upwards. Soften the eyes and come into an easy rhythm of breath.

As you breathe, begin to imagine that you are projecting a barrier of boundaries from the palms of the hands, like a forcefield. Imagine this boundary surrounding your whole body...front...sides...and back. Perhaps this barrier has a color...a texture...even a physical sensation. Allow your breath to solidify this barrier of healthy boundaries. Nothing will move past this barrier. Remain here for six more breaths.

Inhale and on the exhale, stretch the arms out to the side and straighten them. Allow the palms to remain flat. Inhale and bring the hands back into Svasti mudrā. Again, exhale and stretch the arms out, expanding your healthy boundaries. Inhale and come back to the mudrā. Exhale and expand those boundaries. Continue the movement, but this time add the sound of "ram" to give the boundaries even more strength. Inhale... "ram.". See that barrier getting brighter. Inhale... "ram." Once more, strong boundaries. Inhale... "ram."

Keep the arms stretched out wide to the sides. Imagine that this boundary is thick, yet permeable, so that support, love, care, flows through to reach you. Take three breaths with the arms nice and open.

On the next inhale, bring the arms up over the head, leaving space between the palms. Imagine the seed of your spiritual intention in between the hands. See this seed nourished by your practice thus far. Using the sound of "om" draw the hands down into prayer position at the heart. Take three more breaths with your spiritual intention.

Release the hands down into the lap. Sense the left palm and fingers. Sense the right palm and fingers. Feel how the breath is moving in the body. Retain the visualization of your healthy boundaries as you move into your day. Know that these boundaries are here to protect you at any time you need.

Self-Inquiry Questions/Writing Prompts:

- How do you experience healthy boundaries?
- What does it mean and feel like when you are protected? How can you support yourself in connecting with these feelings?

Abhaya Varada – Gesture of Courage

Abhaya means "absence of fear," and varada means "granting wishes." This mudrā combines these two elements to grant the wishes of strength and courage in the face of challenges. With the left hand below the navel we connect with the grounding, centered, fearless qualities of earth energy. With the right palm facing out, we send this energy forward in space and time.

Experience: The Gesture of Courage

Come into a position where the spine can be long extended. Lightly cup both hands. Bring the left hand just below the navel with the palm facing up. Raise the right hand to the level of the right shoulder with the palm facing forward. Allow the right elbow to be near the body, with the forearm perpendicular to the earth. Let the breath settle into an easy rhythm.

Feel the hips grounding into the earth. Experience a sense of groundedness through the hips, the legs, and the feet. Become aware of the breath expanding into the lower abdomen. Invite yourself to join the body and the breath in this moment. Take three breaths here.

Sense into the right palm and imagine a warmth or light in the palm. This is the energy of courage and strength. Imagine that you are projecting this energy of courage and strength out from the palm, like a beam of light. Send this energy of courage and strength forward in your life to a time when you need strength and courage. You do not need to know the particulars of this event, just that there will come a time when you need strength and courage. Imagine you are receiving this boost of strength and courage in the future; filling you up so that you can stand steady and strong in the face of challenges. Let's intensify this energy of strength and courage with three rounds of the tone "ram." Inhale… "ram." Imagine the energy growing stronger. Inhale… "ram." Send that strength and courage to your future self. Inhale… "ram.". Take three more breaths sending this courage and strength forward in time.

Now turn your hand behind you and imagine projecting this energy of courage and strength back in time to a version of yourself that needed it most. Imagine this version of yourself receiving this energy and courage. Give this energy more strength with three rounds of the tone of "ram." Inhale… "ram." Imagine the energy growing stronger. Inhale… "ram." Send that strength and courage to your future self. Inhale… "ram.". Take three more breaths sending this courage and strength back in time.

Bring your right hand to rest on your heart to give yourself some strength and courage right now. Use one long "ram" to feed and fill your heart with this energy. Inhale… "ram." Feel the hand resting on the heart.

Imagine the warmth of the energy of courage and strength filling you up, right here, right now. Take three more breaths to receive this light.

When you finish your third breath, release the hands into the lap. Sense the palms of the hands, left palm and right palm. Perhaps there is warmth in the hands. Sense the right shoulder, perhaps it is a little more awake. Sense yourself; perhaps you are feeling a stronger and more courageous—ready to face the challenges of life. When you're ready allow the eyes to open.

Self-Inquiry Questions/Writing Prompts:

- What does courage and strength mean to you?
- How do you experience courage?
- How do you feel after this practice?

Boundaries: Saying Yes to Saying No

Boundaries are an invisible bubble that we put around our bodies, energies, emotions, thoughts, personal lives, time, space, belongings, friendships, relationships, etc. They protect us from over-expending ourselves. With healthy boundaries, we have increased self-esteem, emotional and mental wellness, and more independence. When they have been crossed, or in some cases pulverized, we can get leaky boundaries. When we have leaky boundaries, we have a hard time saying no. We may feel violated or trampled upon but feel wrong in communicating those feelings.

Establishing boundaries is about knowing our rights and setting limits. We need to be in touch with our feelings and a sense of self-esteem to be able to stand up and say no when something crosses our line. How many of us feel comfortable doing that? This discomfort increases when we are struggling with a trauma history.

Personal questions from strangers about our lives, weight, appearance, finances, etc., cross boundaries. Someone who asks those questions of us has unhealthy boundaries. If we feel uncomfortable with the question, yet answer it anyway, we may have unhealthy boundaries. Someone asking a woman if she is pregnant because her belly seems bigger is crossing boundaries. Asking why a couple has no children, or when they will have children, is crossing boundaries. Venting about your struggles and everything that is going wrong without asking permission to do so, is crossing energetic boundaries. Touch without permission, compliments and comments about appearance, is crossing boundaries.

In many ways, trauma is an event that crosses boundaries, especially in the case of assault and abuse of any kind. When our boundaries get crossed by the people that we love, we can lose our sense of our boundaries. It takes work to re-establish and strengthen those boundaries. We may need to spend some time identifying our limitations again. Working with a mental health professional support us in finding clarity around our boundaries. Below you will find a practice that helps with saying yes to saying no.

Self-inquiry questions/writing prompts:

- This is what I am saying "no" to in my life.
- This is what I am saying "yes" to in my life.

Experience: Healthy Boundaries (5 – 10 minutes)

You will need a space where you can stand with the legs wide apart and make some noise. This practice includes the healthy boundaries mudrā from above with a bhāvanā for strength. It is empowering and encourages taking back your space. That said, if you feel you have struggled with boundaries or a lack of self-esteem and personal power, this may bring up emotions. If that happens, bless those emotions and keep going!

- *Stand with the feet wider apart than the hips with the toes in line with the knees.*
  - o *Bend your knees coming into a wide-legged squat, to check for comfort in the knees, hips, and low back. Adjust if you feel discomfort in any of those areas.*
- *Take a moment here to identify a bhāvanā for strength.*
  - o *This could be a feeling in the body, an image from nature, or your life, or it could be the word strength.*
- *Take three breaths with this bhāvanā, letting it permeate your entire awareness.*
- *Inhale and bring the arms out to the sides in a 5-pointed star.*

- *Exhale with the sound "dhee-ree-ha!!" as you bend your elbows at a 90-degree angle and the*

knees at a 90-degree angle. This is Victory Salute.

- *Inhale back into 5-pointed star, exhale with "dhee-ree-ha!!" into victory salute.*
- *Do this 12 – 15 times really calling out the sound, maybe even yelling it.*
  - o *If we were together in person, I would make you do it louder.*
- *After your last time, come into the victory salute and hold the position.*
- *Practice three rounds of Lion's Breath here.*
  - o *Stick out your tongue, toward your chin, roll your eyes up towards your forehead, roar like a lion from the back of the throat.*
  - o *Roar it out, scaring away anything in your life that is constricting you or holding you back.*
- *Keeping the elbow bent, take your right arm across your body with the palm facing out. Cross the left arm in front with the palm facing out for Svasti Mudrā.*

- *Imagine that the strength you have awoken with your practice coalesces into an energy force at the centers of the palms. Imagine projecting that energy out around your body in a bubble, like a force field.*

- *Take three breaths in this force field, imagining those strong boundaries around you.*

- *Inhale and on the exhale reach your arms out to the sides making the bubble of boundaries bigger around you. Making more space for you within your boundaries.*

- *Inhale and bring the arms back into Svasti mudrā. Exhale and extend the arms.*

- *Repeating this process, add the sound ram (pronounced "rum") three times giving those boundaries more strength.*

- *Change the sound to "yes" on the exhale. Saying yes to giving yourself healthier boundaries. Do this three times.*

- *Change the sound to "no" on the exhale. Saying no to what is no longer serving you in your life. Do this three times.*

- *Take six more movements to use any combination of "ram," yes, or no, supporting those strong and healthy boundaries.*

- *At the end of the sixth breath, hold your arms out to your sides and begin to push in all directions, making those boundaries bigger. Give yourself more space withing your boundaries. You are allowed to take up space! You deserve to take up space!*

- *When you feel complete, inhale with the arms wide and exhale the hands into Lotus Mudrā at the heart to bring a self-compassion into this practice.*

- o *The heels of the hand, thumbs, and pinky fingers touch, with the middle three fingers extended up.*
- *Use the sound yam (pronounced yum) three times here.*

- *Inhale back into 5-pointed star and exhale bring the feet together, releasing the arms down to the sides.*
- *Pause here, keeping the eyes soft. Feel the strength awake in your legs. The feet are grounded on the Earth. Notice the palms of the hands and the fingers. Feel your breath moving in the body. Become aware of the forcefield of your boundaries, stronger and more defined.*
- *Use this practice whenever you need to connect with your internal strength.*
- *You can also practice with this video:* yogafordepression.com/practice-healthy-boundaries/

Self-Inquiry Questions/Writing Prompts:

- My bhāvanā for strength is:
- After this practice, I feel:

The Crown Jewels of Yoga

Nonduality is at the heart of LifeForce Yoga. It is the experience of transcending the realm of opposites into "oneness," or purusha. Nonduality can be found in Buddhism, Hinduism, and other schools of thought. The school of Advaita Vedanta that informs LifeForce Yoga, is a spiritual path to realization, that literally translates to "not two." It is the belief that the only true thing that exists is the Self, or pure consciousness, and everything else is an illusion. Yoga Nidra and directing awareness are ways in which we incorporate nonduality into the practice of LifeForce Yoga. We have a couple of other techniques, but those only happen during weekend workshops and our five- and seven-day programs.

Nondual has become a buzz word for oneness and blissing out. The clinging to oneness has led to shirking the challenges of life. Individuals use the experience of nondual to not have the difficult discussions, feelings, or conflicts that arise. This is called Spiritual Bypassing, which is when someone else's struggles remind us of our own and this makes us uncomfortable. Rather than feel our feelings, we try to fix our feelings by fixing the other person. Having healthy boundaries can support us in feeling our feelings and being able to say, "I am sorry that is happening to you." Nondual is a way to experience our innate wholeness beyond the constrictions of the ego and preferences. It is a time to connect with the part of us that is so much more and to bring this awareness into the world as wisdom.

Directing Awareness: A Mini Yoga Nidra

Directing Awareness is the practice we engage in after the practices. We do it to anchor our minds in the experience and aftereffects of each practice. This keeps the mind focused on the internal landscape and strengthens our self-awareness. In a one-on-one setting or in a yoga class, the LifeForce Yoga Practitioner guiding you through the practices leads the directing awareness. When you practice on your own, you have to do it for yourself, which can be a challenge.

Directing awareness strengthen the muscle of body/emotional awareness. We are better able to see red flags arising before it happens. For example, feelings of overwhelm, exhaustion, and even triggers. An affirmation that exemplifies this is, "from my center, I can identify what I need."

Directing awareness between sides of any poses helps us to be uncomfortable without giving in to the **need** or **desire** to fix. Discomfort is a natural part of the human experience that is inescapable. When we can allow discomfort, we can better regulate impulses. An affirmation that exemplifies this is, "I'm okay when everything is NOT okay."

Directing awareness after a balance pose, sensing into the samenesses, teaches us to remain in our center when everything in our life is going well. Some of us struggle with things going well, we are waiting for the other shoe to drop. Sometimes there is no other shoe. Anchoring the awareness in the experience of balance helps with self-sabotaging behaviors. An affirmation that exemplifies this is, "I remain centered when everything is okay."

Nothing we do on the yoga mat exists in isolation; we are practicing for ease in our daily lives. Every little nuance of a yoga practice supports mental and emotional health. You do not need to be aware of how the practice is acting on the subtleties for it to work.

Here are some tips for when to direct your awareness.
- Start with directing to specific areas of the peripheral physical body, then moving to breath, and eventually to energy, expansiveness, etc.

- When to direct your own awareness:
    - After every breathing practice.
        - After bee breath, we direct the awareness to stillness, silence, etc.
    - After a breath retention.
    - After a flow of movement.
    - After a pose on one side, before moving to the other side.

Yoga Nidra

The heart of yoga is yoga nidra. It is a meditation practice that is done in a lying down position. It can be practiced in a seated position as well. Yoga Nidra takes the awareness and rotates it through the five bodies to get to an experience of our Inner Radiance. When we bring our awareness to any sensation and practice unconditional listen, that sensation will guide us to our wholeness. As Rumi wrote, "the bandaged places are where the light shines through." Yoga nidra is an essential practice and I encourage you to practice it every day. You will find deep healing, rest, ease, and rejuvenation.

While it is possible to guide yourself through the practice, it is best when listening to a recording. To practice, record yourself reading the script below, or practice with a free recording on our website: yogafordepression.com/lifeforce-yoga-nidra-gift. There are many wonderful resources for yoga nidra including two books from Julie Lusk with scripts.

There is a lot to be said about the practice of yoga nidra and our purpose in this manual is to explore options. Therefore, we will touch upon the very basics of yoga nidra. Our online training, Sacred Rest: Yoga Nidra is an excellent way to learn more about yoga nidra as well as how to guide someone else through the practice. The basic process of a LifeForce Yoga nidra:

- Setting an intention for the practice.
- Connecting with your heart felt prayer or spiritual intention.
- Establishing the Inner Sanctuary.
- Sensing the body.
- Sensing the breath.
- Sensing into opposites of feelings.
- Sensing into opposites of emotions and beliefs.
- Experiencing bliss.
- Experiencing the oneness that is your Inner Radiance.
- Connecting with your heart felt prayer or spiritual intention.
- Waking up.

The language and process of LifeForce Yoga Nidra is formulated for supporting mental health. There are many other forms of yoga nidra. The differences you will encounter are that we do not give imagery or affirmations during the practice. The language we use is meant to be inclusive and sensitive to depression, anxiety, and trauma. LifeForce Yoga Nidra is closely aligned with iRest, developed by Richard Miller.

Experience: Yoga Nidra (20 – 25 minutes)

Note: This script was developed for a treatment center and does not include and specific yoga language. The best way to practice this yoga nidra is to record this script in your own voice, making sure to read at a slow and even pace. If you feel that is inaccessible, visit the LifeForce Yoga Store, yogafordepression.com/store to download the *Meditative Relaxation* mp3.

Setting yourself up for meditative relaxation. Feel free to use a chair or your mat on the floor. Prop up the head with a cushion. If the low back feels uncomfortable place the lower legs in a chair, or bend the knees placing the feet flat, wider apart than the hips, so that you can relax the legs. As you settle in, there may be times during this practice where you fall asleep or consciousness seems to wander. If that happens, allow my voice to be like an anchor that keeps you present in the practice and this moment. Snoring may arise. If it does, inquire into who is the one that is snoring.

During this practice, we welcome every sensation, feeling, emotion, and thought, as a doorway to a deeper experience of being present, here and now. Invite your intention, your heartfelt prayer. This is the seed that you, your heart, God, or your higher power, is planting for your personal growth and well-being. It is something that you hope to gain as a result of your practice. Imagine it as true and already happening, right now… Let it go and watch how it returns to you during your practice, during your day. Take a moment to adjust yourself so that you feel ten to fifteen percent more comfortable.

Let's cultivate the inner sanctuary. Your inner sanctuary is the place, real or imagined, where when you go there you feel peaceful, serene and at ease. This could be a place in nature, a special room, maybe the way you feel when you hear your favorite song. If more than one place is a rising, pick one that feels the most resonant or combining all of these places into one super sanctuary. Imagine yourself in your inner sanctuary right now. Begin to take in the sights, sounds, the feeling of your inner sanctuary. Feel yourself becoming more peaceful, more serene, and at ease. This inner sanctuary is available to you at any point during the practice and your daily life when you need peace, serenity, and ease.

Now we'll rotate awareness through the body beginning with the mouth. Sense the lips, the mouth, roof of the mouth, floor of the mouth, sidewalls left and right. Sense the tongue. Experience the whole mouth as sensation. Since the left ear and inner ear canal. Sense the right ear and inner ear canal. Make the mind big enough to experience both ears at the same time. The tip of the nose. Left nostril and right nostril. Sense the left eye, eyebrow, temple, and cheekbone. Sense the right eye, eyebrow, temple, and cheekbone. Expand the mind, the awareness, to experience both eyes at the same time. Sense the forehead, scalp, back the neck, sides of the neck, left and right, and the throat. Experience the whole face, head, neck, and throat as a radiant sensation.

Sense the left side of the body. Whole left side of the body lying on the earth. Left shoulder, elbow, wrist palm, and all the left fingers. Even aware of the space between the fingers. Back of the left hand, forearm, upper arm, and armpit. Experience the whole left arm. Even aware of the energy that surrounds the left arm. Sensing left shoulder blame, left side of the ribs cage, the front, side, and back. Left side of the abdomen and low back. Left hip, knee, ankle, sole of the left foot, and all the left toes. Even aware of the space between the toes. Top of the left foot, lower leg, thigh, and buttock. Experience the whole left leg. Even becoming aware of the energy surrounding the left leg. Experience the whole left side of the body. The whole left side of the body awake in the field of awareness.

And now imagine that the breath travels in for the sole of the left foot, up through the left side of the body all the way to the crown of the head. On the exhale, the breath travels down from the crown of the head, down the right side of the body all the way to the right foot. Every inhale, breath travels in through left. Every exhale, out through right. Inhaling left to the crown of the head. Exhaling right to the sole of the foot. Inhaling left. Exhaling right. Awareness traveling from the left hemisphere of the body to the right hemisphere of the body.

Pouring awareness into the right side of the body. Let go of the breath and sense the right shoulder, right elbow, wrist, palm and all the right fingers. Even aware of the space between the fingers. Back of the right hand, forearm, upper arm, and armpit. Experience the whole right arm. Even aware of the energy that surrounds the right arm. Right shoulder blade, right side of the rib cage, the front, side, and back. Right side of the abdomen and low back. Right hip, knee, ankle, sole of the right foot and all the right toes. Even becoming aware of the space between the toes. Top of the right foot, lower leg, thigh, and buttock. The experience the entire right leg. Even aware of the energy that surrounds the right leg. Experiencing the whole right side of the body, lying on the earth. Whole right side of the body an experience of vibrant and radiant sensation. The whole body and experience of radiant sensation. The whole body breathing itself in and out.

Expand the awareness to experience the whole body. Stepping back into the field of awareness, where these changing the physical sensations raise and fall. Yet awareness is so much more.

Bringing awareness back into the physical body, welcome an area and discomfort. An unpleasant sensation or a tightness. Resist the urge to adjust or fix. Welcome the experience discomfort in the physical body. Breathing and experiencing discomfort in the physical body. Out of this discomfort in the body, an experience of comfort in the physical body. Welcome an area of comfort in the physical body. A pleasant a sensation or a relaxation. Resist the urge to expand or change comfort in the physical body. Instead breathe with comfort in the physical body.

Coming back to discomfort in the physical body. Diving even deeper into discomfort. Perhaps there is an emotion woven into this experience of discomfort in the physical body. No need to search, or analyze, simply welcome and breathe with any emotion that is present within the experience of discomfort in the physical body. Be and breathe with discomfort and any emotion. Moving back into comfort in the physical body. Dive deeper into the experience of comfort and perhaps there is an emotion woven into this experience. No need to search or dig. Simply welcome an emotion if one is present. Be and breathe with any emotion that is woven into this experience of comfort in the physical body. Shifting awareness back to discomfort and any emotion that is present. Breathing with discomfort and emotion. Perhaps insight arises. Shifting back into comfort and any emotion that is present. Be and breathe with comfort and emotion. Perhaps insight arises.

Stepping back into the field of awareness where both discomfort and comfort and their associated emotions exist at the same time. That indescribable and indefinable experience of both at the same time.

Bring the awareness to the heart space. Dive into the heart space and welcome an experience of lightheartedness. Maybe a joyfulness or a blissfulness. Perhaps recalling a memory of lightheartedness. Let the memory go and remain in the experience. Perhaps lightheartedness feels like a warmth spreading through the rib cage, like a smile spreading across the heart. Perhaps a lightness or an openness. Dive deeper into this experience. Feel lightheartedness, joyfulness or blissfulness. Let the whole physical body experience this lightheartedness. Like a smile that spreads through the entire physical body. Feel how the heart expands. The heart expanding into its true nature of loving without exception.

This expanded loving awareness, fully aware of itself. The true nature of awareness, ever present, and unchanging. In this loving awareness, experience yourself as you truly are. Where you are so much more than these changing sensations. So much more than these changing moods, emotions, or thoughts. This loving awareness is your birthright. Within this field of the loving awareness and loving without exception, plant the seed of the heartfelt prayer. Imagine it as true and happening right now.

Sensing the body lying on the earth. Feel the body lying on the earth. This vessel. Take a moment to thank this body for carrying you through this life. Perhaps even sending it a blessing. Feel this body breathing itself, join with this natural rhythm of breath. Begin to deepen the breath. Each breath getting deeper than the last. Begin to awaken the body, wiggling the toes, the ankles, fingers, and the wrists. Begin to reach, stretch and yawn yourself awake. Rolling yourself over onto one side, giving yourself the hug that you have been longing for. You deserve it if for no other reason than because I said so.

Take a moment here before moving to be present with yourself. Noticing how you feel as a result of your practice. Using the support of your top arm, press yourself into a seated position, either on the floor, or in a chair. Let's seal in all the goodness of this practice using sound of Om.

Self-Inquiry Questions/Writing Prompts:

- How do you create space to rest?
- What does the experience of loving awareness feel like for you?

Summary

The experience of trauma displaces our experience of being centered and connected to our Inner Radiance. As a result, we can lose our confidence, boundaries, and our sense of embodiment. Yoga is an exquisite practice in the sense that it invites us to reclaim our connection to our bodies. Using gentle breathing practices and yogic movements strengthens our container and the nervous system, allowing it to heal itself. Adding empowerment techniques brings about a sense of courage and self-esteem. As we begin to establish our strong and healthy boundaries, we can reclaim our space in the world.

LIVING THE EMPOWERED LIFE:
PUTTING IT ALL TOGETHER

You made it! Here we are at the end of our journey together, for now. I hope that you are feeling inspired and the practices are making a difference. If you feel a little overwhelmed with options, not to worry, this is where we put it all together and create a practice.

Commitment to Daily Practice

The only way that yoga works is by committing to a regular practice. Vitamins do not work if you only take them once a week. Yoga does not work if you one practice once a week. Do not get me wrong, going to a yoga class is a great. And we need to do more if we want to stay in connection with our Inner Radiance. In addition to this manual, we have free practices on our website, lots of videos on YouTube including longer practices and online workshops, and audio and video available for purchase in our store. Before we go over guidelines for creating a regular practice, let us do a little self-exploration.

What do I need?

Soften your eyes and ask yourself what you need. Try not to second guess or explain away your first impulses or thoughts.

What do I want out of my practice?

This could be anything. Do not put limitations on a desired end result from your practice.

My three favorite practices for meeting MY mood are:

    1.
    2.
    3.

My three favorite interventions (what calms my mood if I am anxious, or what energizes if I am lethargic) are:

    1.
    2.
    3.

My three favorite practices for balancing and integrating are:

    1.
    2.
    3.

Three practices that I struggled with are:

    1.
    2.
    3.

There are many reasons that we might struggle with a practice. Sometimes that struggle means that we should practice it more. If you struggled because of a caution, do not return to that practice without supervision. If you struggled because you did not like the practice, there might be something there.

How much time do I want to spend on my daily practice?

In a perfect world, how much time do you want to devote to a daily practice for your mental health?

How much time do I have to spend on my daily practice?

Be reasonable, when can you fit practice into your day.

These are the things I am willing to drop so that I can make space for my daily practice.

Think of your practice as how you enhance your life. What are the things that you engage in that detract from your life? What are the time wasters that you do not NEED to engage in?

This is how I will hold myself accountable for my daily practice:

You could leave yourself a note, or schedule it on your calendar. Better yet, find a buddy. This person can help hold you accountable to your commitments to yourself. They are your cheerleader, someone that you can text or call when you do not want to get up and practice. You can do the same for them. You might even be able to create a space where you can practice together.

The LifeForce Yoga 40-Day Challenge

In the beginning stages of the 7-day training, we used to tell people to go home and practice. After 7-days of immersive yoga practices, going home and not doing anything can be like coming off a drug – moods would tank. One year, a practitioner told us that they committed to practicing with one of the DVDs every day for 40 days. They felt better and that they understood the practice. After that, we made it a requirement of the program. Since that time, people tell us how important the 40-Day Challenge is for maintaining a sense of mental health.

40 days seems like a lot. Remember, take it one day at a time. It can also seem overwhelming to fit all the practices in. You do not need to fit all the practices in! Five minutes twice a day can make a significant difference. Start with your favorite practices. Pick one practice that meets your mood, one that is an intervention (alleviates your mood), and one that is balancing. Commit to practicing that for a week. After one week of practice, see how it feels to add in another technique. After another week, maybe adding another practice. And so on. Once you have completed 40 days, start again with another 40 days. Commitment is the most important part. Establishing the habit of practicing for mental health is the second part.

My Commitment to Practice:

Time:
Location:
Practices:

What to Do When Your Mind is Energized and the Body is Tired, or Vice Versa

Things would be so easy if we fit into one of three categories (gunas) – tamas, rajas, and sattva, or depressed, anxious, and balance. Of course, life is not that simple. Instead the often combine to form the complexities that you experience. For example, 80% of people with depression also suffer from anxiety. Hopefully your reading and personal exploration has led to a basic understanding of each guna. If not, feel free to review. This following information is complex and can be confusing, and it can shed a lot of light.

There are nine different basic combinations of the three gunas. They are named after the most prevalent guna. Below you will see the guna combination listed as well as suggestions for meeting the mood, the intervention, and the balancing practice. As you experience more practices, feel free to add your thoughts to the list.

Tamasic tamas	Rajasic tamas	Sattvic tamas
Tamasic rajas	Rajasic rajas	Sattvic rajas
Tamasic sattva	Rajasic sattva	Sattvic sattva

Tamasic tamas

An example of extreme lethargy where there is no energy, like deep delta wave sleep. A person who spends most of their time in a tamasic tamas state might be diagnosed with major depressive disorder, or catatonia.

- Meet the mood: lying down, stair step breath, 4:4 count breath, eyes open, brahma mudrā.
- Mood Interventions: right nostril breathing, bhāvanā for energy, movement, bellows breath, breath of joy, pulling prāna, power hara, and victory salute.
- Balance the mood: moving the breath in the body, alternate nostril and/or yoga nidra.

Rajasic Tamas

An energized lethargy, maybe a mind that is active when the body is exhausted, but with a tendency to be more lethargic than not. Someone who is stuck in this state might receive a diagnosis like anxiety-based depression, or high functioning depression. This form of tamas needs a practice that focuses the mind while meeting the lethargy of the body.

- Meet the mood: lying down or seated, stair step breath, 4:4 count breath, bhāvanā practice, chakra sounds.
- Mood Interventions: LifeForce Yoga Chakra Clearing Meditation, chakra sounds, mudrās.
- Balance the mood: moving the breath in the body, alternate nostril and yoga nidra.

Sattvic Tamas

This is balanced yet in a state of lethargy, an example is shavasana. We might come to this state as a result of our practice before we come to a true state of balance. If you find yourself in this place you do not really need to meet the mood or apply an intervention. In this state, you will find it easier to meditate or be still. The best way to find the practice that you need is to ask yourself what you need. A yoga nidra might be the perfect practice here.

Tamasic Rajas

This a tired energy, like an active body when the mind is tired or active mind/tired body, but with a tendency to be more energetic than not, like exhaustion or in some cases insomnia. Someone who gets stuck in this state might receive a diagnosis of anxiety-based depression (again), high functioning anxiety (knowing that you have anxiety and being able to be calm, or feeling withdrawn), or social anxiety. When someone with PTSD is depressed, this is how their energy might be characterized, it looks like depression, but there is an underlying sensitivity.

- Meet the mood: seated or standing, stair step breath, bhāvanā practice, bouncing, pulling prāna, breath of joy, bellows breath, power hara.
- Mood Interventions: 4:6 count breath, LifeForce Yoga Chakra Clearing Meditation, calming chakra sounds, mudrās.
- Balance the mood: moving the breath in the body, alternate nostril and/or yoga nidra.

Rajasic Rajas

This is an example of energy that is frenetic, hyperactive, and/or hyperarousal. A panic attack or a PTSD triggered state is rajasic rajas. Someone stuck in this state might be given a diagnosis or generalized anxiety disorder, or obsessive-compulsive disorder.

- Meet the mood: standing, bouncing, pulling prāna, breath of joy, power hara, sun salutations, etc.
- Mood Interventions: 4:6 count breath, forward bends, calming sounds, bee breath, left nostril breathing, forward bends.
- Balance the mood: moving the breath in the body, alternate nostril and/or yoga nidra.

Sattvic Rajas

This is an energized balance, an example is how you feel in a movement meditation, or a "runner's/hiker's high." In contrast to the balanced state of lethargy that is sattvic tamas, this is a balanced state of energy. When we are on the rajasic spectrum, we might come to this state as a result of our practice, before we come to a sattvic sattva. Ask yourself what you need when you are in this state.

Tamasic Sattva

This is a calm state of balance. An example might be feeling awake while lying down.

Rajasic Sattva

This is an energized state of balance. An example might be feeling calm while in a standing position.

Sattvic Sattva

This is a state of true balance, it could be called the lightness of being. Examples are meditation, yoga nidra where the mind is awake and aware, the feeling of being present yet non-reactive. Chapter Six of the Bhagavad Gita says, "the yogi is one whose mind is no longer disturbed by the chaos that surrounds them."

Practice Review
In this review, you will find all the practices covered in this manual.

Practice that Meet the Tamasic Mood

- Lying down
- Seated
- Sankalpa

Interventions for the Tamasic Mood

- Bhāvanā for Energy
- Stair Step Breath
- 4:4 Count Breath
- Energizing Mantras
- In Bed Practice
- Brahma Mudrā
- Garuda Mudrā
- Matangi Mudrā

- Heart openers
- Bellows Breath
- Pulling Prāna
- Breath of Joy
- Power Hara
- Victory Salute

Practices that Balance the Tamasic Mood

- Moving the Breath in the Body
- Alternate Nostril
- Directing Awareness
- Yoga Nidra

A Practice that does all three:

The LifeForce Yoga Chakra Clearing Meditation, energizing version, contains meeting the mood through a seated position, bellows breath and the mudrās and mantras for the intervention, and balancing with meditation. Do not worry about the calming aspects of Bee Breath, as these are mitigated by the mudrās and mantras that follow.

Practices that Meet the Rajasic Mood

- Bellows Breath
- Bouncing
- Pulling Prāna
- Breath of Joy
- Power Hara
- Victory Salute

Interventions for the Rajasic Mood

- Calming mantras
- Bhāvanā for peace
- 4:6 count breath
- Left nostril breathing
- Bee Breath
- Forward bends

- Twisting poses

Practices that Balance the Rajasic Mood

- Moving the Breath in the Body
- Alternate Nostril
- Directing Awareness
- Yoga Nidra

Building Your Practice

The simplest way to build your practice is to identify your mood and your desired outcome. Then select one to three items from the list of practices that meet your mood, one to three items from the interventions list, and one to three from the list of practices that balance. Remember to add techniques as you discover things that work for you.

Example 1: You wake up feeling very tired (tamasic). You meet the mood by lying bed. The interventions are stair step breath with a bhāvanā of being awake. You balance the mood by moving the breath in the body.

Example 2: Your mind is racing, and you are feeling tired. You meet your body's mood by sitting and practice the LifeForce Yoga Chakra Clearing Meditation, the calming version. You mind is being met by the entirety of the practice.

Example 3: It is the middle of the workday and you are tired. You meet your mood by sitting at your desk. The intervention is brahma mudrā. You balance the mood with five minutes of alternate nostril breathing.

Example 4: You just had an intense meeting and you are amped up and cannot focus. You meet your mood by bouncing. The interventions you use are 4:6 count breathing while you bounce, and a standing bhāvanā practice for peace. You balance the mood with moving the breath in the body and a few rounds of alternate nostril breathing.

As you develop a relationship with the practice you will understand what works best for you and when to use it. The most valuable piece of advice I can give you to keep practicing! It makes all the difference in the world.

Thank you for embarking on this journey through LifeForce Yoga with me. May you have the support, the wins, and the ease that you desire.

ABOUT THE AUTHOR

Rose Kress, ERY-500, C-IAYT, Owner/Director of the LifeForce Yoga Healing Institute, is a long-term yoga practitioner, wisdom seeker, and healer. She devotes her life to helping others find the keys to unlocking wellness on all levels of existence. Rose teaches LifeForce Yoga internationally and leads programs online to reduce environmental impact.

Rose lives and teaches yoga in Lebanon, Oregon with her husband of 24 years.

Printed in Great Britain
by Amazon

83497004R00093